IDENTITY CRISIS

Transforming Your Life From Within

—— JACK ALAN HOKE ——

Identity Crisis—Transforming Your Life From Within
   by Jack Alan Hoke
Published by HigherLife Development Services, Inc.
400 Fontana Circle
Building 1—Suite 105
Oviedo, Florida 32765
(407) 563-4806
www.ahigherlife.com

Unless otherwise noted, Scripture quotations are from: NIV—1984.

ISBN 13: 978-1-939183-09-5

Cover Design: Dave Whitlock

First Edition

11 12 13 14 — 9 8 7 6 5 4 3 2 1
Printed in the United States of America

DEDICATION

Dedicated to the body of Christ, the Bride, the beloved children of God.

For my brother, Clayton (Butch) E. Hoke Jr., who is now with the Lord. His prayers helped bring me into the kingdom of God.

Also, to my daughters Lyndsai, Karlee and Abby Hoke.

My love and prayers for you will never cease.

Love, Dad.

—JACK HOKE

TABLE of CONTENTS

ACKNOWLEDGEMENTS

MY THANKS TO the leaders of Christ Community Church, of Camp Hill, PA. I acknowledge Senior Pastor Dave Hess, Pastor Shawn Geraty, Pastor Thom Gardner, Pastor Bob and Zory Klinger, Pastor Herb Stoner, Pastor of Praise and Worship Jeremiah Grube and Pastor of Community Life Tim Sprik, for their love and patience. They enabled me and many others to see into the heart of Christ, equipping the body of Christ to do the work of the saints. Also to Randy Clark, the Apostolic leader of Global Awakening, whose humility has helped many to believe in themselves. Or, as Randy would put it, "God can use little ole me's." Where would we be without those mighty intercessors? Thank you!

Kelly Maria, Lee, Annette, Barbara, Mellisa, Donna, and Debi. You guys are true warriors!

Thank you, Paris and Brenda Willfong for teaching me about character. Above all, I want to give thanks to the Lord Jesus Christ for His love, faithfulness, sense of humor, and the simplicity of knowing Him.

Dear Mom and Dad:

How you stood by me and always believed in me was a miracle in itself. Both of you were the greatest attributes of love I ever knew. Never did either of you keep a record of my wrongs (1 Corinthians 13:5). And, as you said, Mom: "There has to be a God to have changed you, Jack." I'll see you both soon.

Love,
Jack

FOREWORD

By Pastor Chris Maxwell

I REMEMBER MY INITIAL conversation with Jack Hoke. Our previous dialogue had only been through email. But that time, we talked on the phone as I drove along the interstate to the airport in Atlanta, GA. I was looking forward to a trip where I would speak words I hoped would bring life, healing, and hope for the audiences. My dialogue with Jack initiated a discussion that would turn teamwork for a project into a friendship for life. It also let me hear from the heart of someone else who sought to bring life, healing, and hope for a large audience.

As an author, I know the importance of asking questions. During that conversation, I only asked a few. Jack answered those questions. With passion and vision, he answered those questions. With honesty and hopes, he answered those questions. With words of life, he answered those questions.

I agreed with Jack's answers. He believed that many of us face, what he called, an Identity Crisis. He contended that many of us need to experience life transformation from within. But, as a counselor and writer, I wanted to know how. What was his plan? How could those suffering from the status he described find a new way of viewing their identity? How did he know that such a process would work? What did the Bible say about it?

After that conversation, I spent time at the airport and on the plane reading Jack's early draft of *Identity Crisis*. The pages were covered with references and quotes. A biblical text followed another text which followed another. Scripture covered the manuscript. Traveling and wanting to know the direction of his book, I continued reading his collection of topical references, related Scripture and suggestions for a deeper understanding of this Identity Crisis. The pages were many. The more read, I remembered listening to Jack's hope for the book. Then I realized there was a missing piece. On those many pages of deep content, readers needed to know the author. How did the reality of his words and themes fit in his life? I felt audiences in our painful world needed to hear his voice, experience his stories, feel his hurt, and notice his victories.

To make that happen, I boarded a different plane at a different time and flew in a different direction. I spent three days interviewing Jack. The more I asked, the more stories he told. I knew then that *Identity Crisis* could powerfully reveal portions of his stories. The various topics needed fresh revelation—Jack's stories could provide a few sets to help us all get ready to receive the Scripture which would follow.

And now? I believe *Identity Crisis* does that. Each topic invites us to board a plane and travel in a new direction. After boarding our life-planes and taking off with words of defeat and failure, readers can soar and land with victory and success. Negativity can be replaced with transparent accomplishment. Negative self-talk can be silenced and replaced with thoughts of victorious living. Not by denying our hurt. But by relating to stories like Jack tells and moving them toward their new destination.

Notice what luggage you've been carrying for too long. Open these pages and receive the new carry-on bags of truth and freedom. You'll find life, healing, and hope. Then, when you take a glance at yourself, you'll begin noticing a new you. You'll have moved from Identity Crisis to your identity in Christ.

INTRODUCTION

EVEN THOUGH MY parents never divorced, their relationship put the "fun" in dysfunctional. As the youngest of five, it seemed to me that everything flowed downhill. By the age of ten, I believed I could do nothing right. By the age of 13, I began to spiral uncontrollably, involving myself in everything unhealthy to fill the "hole in my soul."

I banged my head on the floor. I wanted someone to hold me. How did my parents respond? With just one question: "What's wrong with you?"

I by no means want to dishonor my parents. Their culture was Pennsylvania Dutch. As I remember, they did the best they could with what they were equipped with. Like the saying, "The fruit doesn't fall far from the tree." With a divorce rate of 50% both inside and outside of the church, our children grow up with a lost identity of not knowing who they are. I know firsthand.

Many things are embedded into the fiber of our character and personality in the first six years of experiencing and reacting to life - attitudes, judgments, and expectations are formed. A child's persona has been deeply ingrained in those initial six years.

In Proverbs, King Solomon said there is life and death in the tongue. Indeed, as parents we have had the power to speak destiny into the formative lives of our children. It is very disheartening that as parents we are not always aware of the power of our speech. Words can crack the foundation of the ones we love so much—our children.

This book will not flow like a novel. It is written and designed for study. But not only study. For healing. When the lies are broken and replaced with truth, we become new.

Identity Crisis is designed to help us seek out our true identity - just as our Heavenly Father sees us through the eyes of His beloved Son Jesus Christ. We as humans have a tendency to press on in terms of managing our behavior, rather than by the renewing of our minds (Rom. 12:2). *Identity Crisis* invites you into that life changing experience of renewing the mind.

The receiving of a new heart and spirit will result in changed behavior (Ps. 51; Ezek. 36:26). Jesus said it happens when we choose to "dig deep" to the foundations of our lives (Luke 6:36-49). Ultimately, every fiber in my being was designed to be filled with the love of God. I don't know your story, but I know this: Every fiber of your being was also designed to be filled with the love of God.

Now is the time to dig deep. Now is the time for the lies to end. Now is the time for the truth to set us free from our past, from our fears, from our self hate. Now is the time to deal with our Identity Crisis. Now is the time to see ourselves through our Father's eyes.

I hope - as you meditate on the following Scriptures, stories, and reflective questions - that the True Identity of who Christ says you are becomes a reality. I pray you truly become a new creation in Christ.

May you be enveloped in His arms of love to fulfill His kingdom purposes here on earth and for all of eternity.

> [7] *Dear friends, let us love one another, for love comes from God. Everyone who loves has been born of God and knows God.* [8] *Whoever does not love does not know God, because God is love.* [9] *This is how God showed his love among us: He sent his one and only Son into the world that we might live through him.* [10] *This is love: not that we loved God, but that he loved us and sent his Son as an atoning sacrifice for our sins.* [11] *Dear friends, since God so loved us, we also ought to love one another.* [12] *No one has ever seen God; but if we love one another, God lives in us and his love is made complete in us (1 John 4:7-12).*

¹⁶ You did not choose me, but I chose you and appointed you so that you might go and bear fruit—fruit that will last—and so that whatever you ask in my name the Father will give you (John 15:16).

⁴ But when the kindness and love of God our Savior appeared, ⁵ he saved us, not because of righteous things we had done, but because of his mercy. He saved us through the washing of rebirth and renewal by the Holy Spirit, ⁶ whom he poured out on us generously through Jesus Christ our Savior, ⁷ so that, having been justified by his grace, we might become heirs having the hope of eternal life (Titus 3:4-7).

CHAPTER ONE:

ADOPTED by GOD

I REMEMBER HOW I got my identity. Not with love and acceptance. Not with forgiveness and joy. Not with hope and healing. I was told so many lies for so many years:

You can't do anything right!

You are stupid!

What is wrong with you?

I was a kid that needed love and attention, and would do anything to get it.

I also remember how I got my new identity. By accepting God's acceptance, I was welcomed into His family. The Heavenly Father – the One who created me in His image, the One who paid a high price to adopt me, the One who promised to always be with me – was my new Dad. To silence the lies from my former life and become joyful instead of bitter, I had to work on getting my identity. Yes, I was accepted freely because Jesus paid the price. But mentally and emotionally grasping who I am in Christ took much prayer and spiritual development.

When I tend to go back to the words which were spoken over me as a child, I choose to silence those lies and believe the truth:

I am loved by my Father in Heaven.

I am blessed, not cursed.

I am highly favored.

I am not stupid!

I have the mind of Christ.

How did you get your identity? What is that former life telling you? What Identity Crisis are you facing? How have you ignored what those around you notice? Are you willing to let God give you a new Identity? Are you willing to believe today that you are made in the image of God?

Identify the lies. Replace them with the truth.

These following passages of Scripture can help you do that. Read and reflect. Think about the lies you believe. Think of how they have influenced your life.

Receive the truth. Receive the new Identity.

So many times we go on our feelings. That is okay as long as our feelings are based on truth. If we believe a lie then we think a lie and feel a lie and live a lie. But now we are choosing to believe truth.

ADOPTION

So in Christ Jesus you are all children of God through faith (Galatians 3:26).

Adoption is the bestowing of son-or-daughter status to a person who does not hold that title by blood. Typically in Scripture, we see three different types of adoption mentioned: Natural—Pharaoh's daughter adopted Moses (Ex. 2:10) and Mordecai adopted Esther (Est. 2:7); National—God adopted Israel (Ex. 4:22; Deut. 7:6; Hos. 11:1; Rom. 9:4); and finally, Spiritual—Jesus' atoning work on the cross brings men and women into the family of God (John 17:23; Rom. 5:5-8). He can call us sons and daughters because of Jesus.

Are you living as a child of God?

_____

_____

_____

APPLE OF HIS EYE

> *¹⁰ In a desert land he found him, in a barren and howling waste. He shielded him and cared for him; he guarded him as the apple of his eye (Deuteronomy 32:10).*

> *⁸ Keep me as the apple of your eye; hide me in the shadow of your wings (Psalm 17:8).*

Being the "apple" of someone's eye is an English idiom denoting affection. If we are the apple of God's eye, it means He cherishes us and watches over us ceaselessly. We are forever in His focus, the object of His protective love. In the Old Testament, God proved to Israel that they were the "apple of His eye" by giving them war victories (Ex. 17: 8-13), food (Ex. 16:31), and even much needed chastisement (Amos 5:21-24). In this New Testament age, God has proven that we are the "apple of His eye" through Jesus' sacrifice on the cross (John 3:16) and by giving us His Holy Spirit to dwell with us (John 15:26).

What does it mean to be cherished?

_____

_____

_____

FIRST FRUITS

> *¹⁸ He chose to give us birth through the word of truth, that we might be a kind of first fruits of all he created (James 1:18).*

In the Hebrew sacrificial system, the initial harvest and the firstborn livestock were considered "first fruits." They were sacrificed to God in acknowledgement of His ownership of the Earth. When the Hebrews gave God their bounty, He blessed them and the rest of their farming endeavors. The firstborn sons also had a special significance: they inherited their father's estate (Deut. 21:15-17; Isa. 61:7) and the paternal blessing (Gen. 27). Because God adopts us as sons and daughters, we are, in a sense, firstborns. We have a blessing and an inheritance, but we also must sacrifice ourselves, and our former lives, to become His.

Is there anything you need to lay at the altar?

_____

_____

_____

FOLLOWERS OF GOD

> [1] *Follow God's example, therefore, as dearly loved children (Ephesians 5:1).*

Jesus' disciples literally followed Him long miles, even up mountains. Today, life is still full of winding roads. We all must walk along mountains of accomplishment, valleys of depression, and rivers of unpredictability. Without an example to guide us, we would be utterly lost. We need someone to learn from. As a child imitates his parents, a believer should imitate God (Matt. 5:48; Luke 6:36). But how can we know who God is? We can't – unless we know Jesus. Jesus' sacrificial love is what we are to follow in our daily lives, regardless of circumstance. By following Him, we find a better way. He is our trailblazer – and because He loves us, He won't leave us on the wayside (Matt. 28:20b).

Where do you think Jesus is leading you?

_____

_____

_____

MY NEW IDENTITY

Take time to study and contemplate the topics you have read. Which biblical image stood out to you? Consider the following questions and pray these prayers. Allow God to meet with you as you rediscover who He has created you to be.

- What lies have been spoken over you regarding your identity?

- What truths have been revealed to you through this chapter?

A prayer for those who spoke lies to us: *Father, forgive them. Like me, they have made mistakes. Please give them a new identity. Help them to let go of the past.*

A prayer for ourselves: *Father, thank You for making me the apple of Your eye, a cherished child. Help me see myself as You see me.*

Spend time in joyful worship, celebrating His acceptance, His love. Celebrate today – no matter what else is occurring in your life. God has adopted you!

CHAPTER TWO:

FRIEND of GOD

G OD LOVES US. Those three words can change our lives forever. If we fail to receive the reality of those three words, we miss out on experiencing a wonderful relationship with a mighty God.

So often, too many other things take the place of God's love. Stuff enters our lives and begins robbing us of the reality we need and crave most: a true, ongoing, never ending friendship with God. I know from personal experience. From my childhood until I was 35, I had such a hole in my soul that I would do anything for attention. I wanted to feel important, to feel needed.

Using drugs. Selling drugs. Fornication. Lies. Deception. Addiction. Anger. I was trying to fill my soul with love, but I was actually filling my soul with more hurt. Hurt to myself and to those around me. My responses to hurt and loneliness led to more hurt and loneliness.

I needed a friend. I needed God as my friend.

I didn't know about true love. I thought sex was love. So, what happened? I started reading Scripture. Passages like those which cover these pages. Verses of truth. Chapters of love and hope and a friendship with God.

My life had been missing out on what I needed the most. I was amazed when I read about love in the Bible – real love. I didn't know how to give or receive love. The lies had deceived me for so long. The revelation of His love began a transformation that continues to this day. I began a vibrant friendship with a Holy God.

What have you substituted for God's love? 1 Corinthians 13 revealed to me the true love I wanted. That was a life changing encounter.

If we choose to live this life of a friendship with God, we can receive His love. We can then pass that love along to others. We can live that 1 Corinthians 13 life. Receiving His love and giving His love. Receiving His love and giving His love. Receiving His love and giving His love. It is an ongoing experience. It doesn't have to end. It is there and real, no matter what we are facing. No matter how we feel.

That is a great lifestyle, but one that too many people miss. Let's not miss it. Let's experience the friendship with God.

Have you received His love? Have you chosen to give it away to people in need? Let's share God's friendship with others – not with the best dressed or best looking or most popular. Give away His love to those who are sad, to those desperate for a true divine friendship, to those craving God's love. Keep your eyes open to God, but also to those around you who are desperate for this friendship. God will draw you closer to Him and He will direct you to others.

FRIEND OF GOD

> [23] And the scripture was fulfilled that says, "Abraham believed God, and it was credited to him as righteousness," and he was called God's friend (James 2:23).

The more we learn and understand about God, the more startling it is that He considers us a "friend." The supreme, ageless, all-powerful Creator of the universe knows we exist! And even more puzzling – He wants to live in us. We're His favored companions. Let's consider these truths about God, and then embrace the fact He desires our friendship:

• God is self-sufficient (Ps. 50:10-12).

- God is eternal (Deut. 33:27; Ps. 90:2).

- God is wise (Prov. 3:19; 1 Tim. 1:17).

- God is sovereign (Isa. 46:9-11).

- God is incomprehensible (Job 11:7-19; Rom. 11:33).

- God is righteous and just (Ps. 119:137).

- God is faithful (Deut. 7:9; Ps. 89:1-2).

- God is light (James 1:17; 1 John 1:5).

- God is merciful (Ps. 103:8-17).

- God is gracious (Ps. 111:4; 1 Peter 5:10).

- God is love (John 3:16; Rom. 5:8).

What aspect of God is most difficult for you to accept?

_____

_____

_____

CHILDREN OF THE KINGDOM

The field is the world, and the good seed stands for the people of the kingdom. The weeds are the people of the evil one (Matthew 13:38).

When Jesus lived on Earth, most people were farmers. So when He spoke of seeds and weeds, the audience caught the message. God's people grow. The children of the Kingdom of God are good seeds. They are flourishing creatures. Those who reject God are stifled by their own insecurities and selfishness. They choke the seeds that want to multiply. We must work through our own self-centeredness, allowing God to heal us, so that we can grow and help others grow.

Are you allowing God to grow within?

_____

_____

_____

SAVED BY THE LORD

> [29] *Blessed are you, Israel! Who is like you, a people saved by the LORD? He is your shield and helper and your glorious sword. Your enemies will cower before you, and you will tread on their heights (Deuteronomy 33:29).*

"*Natan,*" a verb that means "to deliver" in Hebrew, appears over *2,000* times in the Bible in a few different forms. God is in the business of saving! He saved Noah from the flood (Gen. 6:17-18). He freed the Israelites from slavery in Egypt (Ex. 12:31-42). He spared King David from Saul (1 Sam. 23:14). He protected Rahab and her family in Jericho (Josh. 6:25). He rescued Peter from prison (Acts 12:5-10). He saved Paul from stoning (Acts 14:19-20), shipwreck (Acts 27:27-44), and snakes (Acts 28:3-6). Those are just a few instances—the ultimate example, of course, is that Jesus died to save us all from sin and death.

Is there anything you need saving from today?

_____

_____

_____

MY NEW IDENTITY

Take time to study and contemplate the topics you have read. Which biblical image stood out to you? Consider the following questions and pray these prayers. Allow God to meet with you as you rediscover who He has created you to be, in light of who *He* is.

- Have you been guilty of "creating God in your own image," or, rather, projecting your biases on Him?

- How can you grow in friendship with God?

A prayer for the friends who have failed us: *Lord, forgive them. Like me, they have made mistakes. Please remind them of Your friendship. Help us to let go of the past.*

A prayer for ourselves: *Lord, thank yYou for making me Your friend, a sought-after companion. Help me see myself as You see me.*

Spend time in joyful worship, celebrating His acceptance, His friendship. Celebrate today – no matter what else is occurring in your life. God has befriended you!

CHAPTER THREE:

BLESSED by GOD

W E OFTEN FORGET how God has blessed us. Our circumstances and our situations control our moods. God's truth doesn't show up in our feelings or our thoughts. We dwell on what isn't "going just right" instead of taking action on finding a positive blessing in the middle of our pain.

Speaking of pain, I know about it. I feel pain every moment of every day.

Since my fall and surgeries, I cannot move my neck downward to read. To read Scripture, I needed to listen to an audio. But that wasn't best for me. I wanted to read and chew on His Word. This was a major problem.

So I purchased an iPad. My neighbor came up with a device where I could use my iPad over my head – reading Scripture while lying down! The device moves up and down, left and right. I can stay in bed to support the neck and lower back while looking up at the promises of God. I can rest in His Word, pray in His Word, and not struggle to lift my neck up.

What is your major problem? What keeps you from seeing God's promises and believing His blessings?

Put God's Word before your eyes of faith. See His truth – no matter what else is staring back at you. If you need to find a new way of reading or listening or hearing or taking notes or believing, then find that way. Refuse to let your present problems rob you of God's goodness.

Even in your areas of pain and disappointment, even through your struggles and poor decisions, have faith today. Believe you are blessed by God.

Rest and look up. Whether or not you have a literal sign over your head, see through the eyes of faith. Believe His promises. Take Him at His Word.

Rest in His Word. Pray in His Word. As you read and study these biblical texts, receive what God is saying to you. Believe God is lifting you up. You are blessed – right now, no matter your situation – by Father God.

BLESSED

> *[1] Blessed is the one whose transgressions are forgiven, whose sins are covered (Psalm 32:1).*

In Scripture, being "blessed" has a few different connotations: when applied to God ("Bless the Lord"), it has a sense of praise; when used by humans ("Blessed am I"), it can indicate a sense of congratulatory happiness. That happiness, however, is not dependent on material bounty as much as it is on an inner-contentment found in relationship with God. But being blessed is still often confused with having wealth.

Consider this quote from one African native on the subject: "Americans seem to expect that everything will be provided for them. For us, this ear of corn is a gift from God. This evening's rain is a shower of mercy upon us. This healthy breath is life giving. And maybe tomorrow we will not have such things, but our hearts are so full from God..." (*Hope in the Dark*, Jeremy Cowart & Jana Lee 2006)

What does the word "blessing" mean to you?

_____

_____

_____

BLAMELESS

> *⁷ Therefore you do not lack any spiritual gift as you eagerly wait for our Lord Jesus Christ to be revealed. ⁸ He will also keep you firm to the end, so that you will be blameless on the day of our Lord Jesus Christ (1 Corinthians 1:6-8).*

As the old saying goes, "nobody's perfect." And yet, in the Bible, we see that Jesus *is* perfect (Heb. 2:10; 5:9; 7:28). He was without blame. And because of His perfection and sacrifice, we become blameless in God's sight when we accept His salvation. No matter what you've done, no matter who you've hurt or who has hurt you—when you accept Jesus, your un-perfect self begins the divine process of maturity, wholeness, and purity that culminates in the life to come (Phil. 3:9-11).

Are you being responsible with the grace God has bestowed to you?

_____

_____

_____

POOR & LOWLY

> *⁶ Though the LORD is exalted, he looks kindly on the lowly; though lofty, he sees them from afar (Psalm 138:6).*

> *³⁴ He mocks proud mockers but shows favor to the humble and oppressed (Proverbs 3:34).*

> *³ Blessed are the poor in spirit, for theirs is the kingdom of heaven. ¹¹ Blessed are you when people insult you, persecute you and falsely say all kinds of evil against you because of me (Matthew 5:3,11).*

Poverty is categorized in two ways in the Bible: moral poverty (which can result in laziness and loss of wealth), and poverty that is the result of injustice (Prov. 13:23). As the story of Moses illustrates, God can use the odd and awkward to do His work of liberating the oppressed (Ex. 4:10-12). God freeing the Israelites from Pharaoh is presented as a great exemplar of God's justice to the needy (Ps. 68:5-10; Exod. 2:23-24). He longs to bless the poor and downtrodden.

Consider this quote from musician and humanitarian Bono: "God is in the slums, in the cardboard boxes where the poor play house. God is in the silence of a mother who has infected her child with a virus that will end both their lives. God is in the cries heard under the rubble of war... and God is with us if we are with them."

God hears the cries of the poor (Psalm 12:5). If you are in need, know that God is on your side.

MY NEW IDENTITY

Take time to study and contemplate the topics you have read. Which biblical image stood out to you? Consider the following questions and pray these prayers. Allow God to meet with you as you rediscover who He has created you to be and as you consider His blessings.

- Take a moment to "count your blessings." What has God blessed you with?

- Are you sharing your blessings with others?

A prayer for the needy: *Lord, give peace and contentment to those who struggle. Remind them that You are the ultimate blessing.*

A prayer for ourselves: *Lord, thank you for blessing me with Your presence. Help me find happiness in You, even when life is difficult. Help me see myself as You see me.*

Spend time in joyful worship, celebrating His acceptance, His blessing. Celebrate today – no matter what else is occurring in your life. God has blessed you!

CHAPTER FOUR:

HABITATION of GOD

WHO DOES GOD say that you are?

During my seasons of change, of adjusting, of becoming aware of weaknesses, of confessing my pain, God showed me that I did not have to perform for His love. That wasn't easy. Yes, it was good news. I needed to hear that and to know it. I needed to receive those words. But becoming aware of this reality and adjusting my lifestyle was a process of spiritual growth and development.

I had been a performance junky. God revealed to me that He loved me where I was, how I was, and who I was. He didn't demand that I change before He was willing to love me. He said, "I love you."

He calls me His son.

He says I am beautiful.

He declares me as blessed, as highly favored.

Think about it. That is my Heavenly Father talking about me. That's Him talking *to* me. Not condemning me. Not abusing me. Not rejecting me. Not waiting until He sees how well I perform.

My Father – my Heavenly Father – loving me. Just loving me.

Having the best Dad in the world is the best way to live in this world. My Father watches over me. He is my friend.

So many times I have tried to earn approval or favor from people.

Searching for the attention of a father or a friend, I tried almost anything. As that began occurring in my relationship with Father God, He said, "Stop. Be still. Receive my love. You have nothing to prove. Just be still. I have chosen to love you and live with you."

That type of true love is so different than what we expect from this world and what we pursue in our self-centered dreams. But that truth – God who knows us and loves us chooses to live within us – reminds me of how we so often seek love from wrong sources and places.

As God's habitation, we can receive relational love. God knowing us. God loving us. God choosing to love with a never ending love.

When have you welcomed God's love? How did you realize performing will not force His love to come your way? Can you grasp an ongoing, never ending love relationship with God?

If so, you become His habitation. You become His dwelling place.

HABITATION OF GOD (OR TEMPLE OF GOD)

22 And in him you too are being built together to become a dwelling in which God lives by his Spirit (Ephesians 2:22).

19 Do you not know that your bodies are temples of the Holy Spirit, who is in you whom you have received from God? You are not your own... (1 Corinthians 6:19).

In the Old Testament, God's Spirit was accessed within the Israelite Temple or the Ark of the Covenant. In order to get close to the "holy of holies," a person had to be a ritually cleansed priest (Lev. 16:17). However, after Jesus died on the cross and rose again, anyone who believes in Him can come into the presence of God. Not only can a person get close—God's spirit will actually live *within* them (1 Cor. 6:19). He is willing to make your heart His habitat.

Have you rolled out the red carpet for God and welcomed Him in?

ELECT

> [22] *"If those days had not been cut short, no one would survive, but for the sake of the elect those days will be shortened (Matthew 24:22).*
>
> [11] *Yet, before the twins were born or had done anything good or bad—in order that God's purpose in election might stand:* [12] *not by works but by him who calls (Romans 9:11-12a).*
>
> [5] *So too, at the present time there is a remnant chosen by grace (Romans 11:5).*

In the New Testament, election concentrates on Jesus Christ as the elect one through whom God achieves His goal of Salvation for all. Through belief in and allegiance to Christ, His followers are elected, or chosen by God. It is a paradox within Christianity – we choose God, but He ultimately chose us.

Do you believe that God wants you?

_____

_____

_____

IMAGE OF GOD

> [26] *Then God said, "Let us make mankind in our image, in our likeness, so that they may rule over the fish in the sea and the birds in the sky, over the livestock and all the wild animals, and over all the creatures that move along the ground.* [27] *So God created mankind in his own image, in the image of God he created them; male and female he created them (Genesis 1:26-27).*

Have you ever felt the urge to create something beautiful? Have you ever experienced anger when injustice occurs in front of you? Do you find joy in your friendships? There is a reason for this! It's because God is creative, hates injustice, and delights in communion with Himself (the Trinity) and His people. Our souls reflect Him because He made us in His image.

Do your actions reflect God's image?

_____

_____

_____

MY NEW IDENTITY

Take time to study and contemplate the topics you have read. Which biblical image stood out to you? Consider the following questions and pray these prayers. Allow God to meet with you as you rediscover who He has created you to be.

- How does it feel to be "chosen" of God?

- If you're body is the Temple of God, is there anything you want to change in your life to honor Him better?

A prayer for the Christians in our lives who have failed to reflect God's image: *Lord, forgive them. They've made mistakes just like me. Fill them with a renewed sense of Your acceptance and Your unmerited favor.*

A prayer for ourselves: *Lord, thank You for making humanity a priority. Thank You for dwelling with us and within us. Help me see myself as You see me.*

Spend time in joyful worship, celebrating His habitation. Celebrate today – no matter what else is occurring in your life. God dwells within you!

CHAPTER FIVE:

BRIDE of CHRIST

WHEN I BECAME aware of this good news, I came out preaching. Quickly. I wasn't prepared for what I was about to experience. There were too many holes I did not know how to fill.

My salvation experience in 1997 was a radical encounter. I immediately could notice the difference between spiritual light and darkness. I saw evil spirits and experienced the visitation of angels. *Once I encountered the pure love of God – it was like the love of Christ was knocking me to the ground with hula-hoops of light.*

Honestly, because of its intensity, I felt like I was going to die.

My kids saw me and said, "Dad, you are glowing." They were young, but they had no doubt that their father had been visited by Jesus.

During those years, I traveled in sales. My spiritual experience filled me with such enthusiasm that I could hardly shut up. I was always preaching while traveling. If I was home, I was in the prayer closet calling out to God or reading the Bible instead of watching television.

At the kids' sports activities or other events, I felt the Holy Spirit all over me. I would open my mouth and He would fill it. Often, though, I said too much.

When I went through personal pain and things stopped feeling so exciting, I had to convince myself that God had not left me. Even if I could not "feel the Spirit" like I had before, did that mean He was gone?

Two things were happening. I was personally experiencing painful life events, and I was also beginning to mature in my faith. Can those things happen at the same time? How are they related?

Rather than basing my relationship with Christ on enthusiasm, God began quietly revealing to me my role as the Bride of Christ. Jesus was the true source of desired Love. Not emotions. Not self-righteousness. Deep, intimate, and true love.

In six years' time, I had a series of accidents resulting in eight spine surgeries. I could no longer work. Through those wounds and disappointments, I had to position myself to choose life as Christ's bride.

Talking and confessing to a counselor helped. He revealed to me the wounds I had inherited, the wounds I had allowed, the wounds I had ignored.

Take time to notice your wounds. I know, we like to avoid that. We tend to live in denial – observing the pain reminds us of hurts we've attempted to defeat. But until our wounds are healed, we are targets. Me? I realized through extensive Christian counseling that I was dysfunctional.

Growing up as the youngest child, I didn't get the love I needed. Due to the German culture I was raised in, coupled with complications at birth, I grew up deeply wounded spiritually, emotionally and mentally.

For me to serve properly as a portion of Christ's body, I needed to be healed myself. For me to believe that I could walk down the aisle as a clean white Bride of Christ, I needed to silence the lies, believe the Word, and receive my healing.

Don't you? Don't you need to be healed from deep, inner hurts?

Visit with the Counselor. Receive the healing you've long awaited. These words – portions of God's Word to us – can powerfully bring healing and prepare you for entering the wedding celebration without carrying the heaviness of past hurt.

BRIDE OF CHRIST

> ² *I saw the Holy City, the new Jerusalem, coming down out of heaven from God, prepared as a bride beautifully dressed for her husband. ...* ⁹*One of the seven angels who had the seven bowls full of the seven last plagues came and said to me, "Come, I will show you the bride, the wife of the Lamb" (Revelation 21:2,9).*

> ¹⁷ *The Spirit and the bride say, "Come!" And let the one who hears say, "Come!" Let the one who is thirsty come; and let the one who wishes take the free gift of the water of life (Revelation 22:17).*

Often in the Epistles, the Church is referred to as the Bride of Christ (2 Cor. 11:2; Eph. 5:25–27, 31f; *cf.* Rev. 19:7; 21:2; 22:17). God is depicted as the divine Bridegroom who pursues His bride passionately and enters into a covenant relationship with her. And no matter what "she" does, He remains faithful. The idea isn't only found in the New Testament—one of the most vivid examples of this concept is found the book of Hosea, in which God is depicted as a jealous lover and Israel a wanton wife!

Are you being faithful to Christ?

FAMILY OF GOD

> ¹⁴ *For this reason I kneel before the Father,* ¹⁵ *from whom every family in heaven and on earth derives its name (Ephesians 3:14-15).*

In the early church, it was considered a virtue to have and support a family (1 Tim. 5:8). Views on family were expanded as the Christian community grew to consider itself a cohesive familial unit (Gal. 6:10; Eph. 2:19); they believed that God was the universal Parent from whom every Christian could claim lineage. As it is with many human families, the Church has since had countless conflicts and divisions. But through it all, we remain united in Christ.

Are you actively ministering to your family?

_____

_____

_____

RANSOMED & REDEEMED

[10] *...and those the LORD has rescued will return. They will enter Zion with singing; everlasting joy will crown their heads. Gladness and joy will overtake them, and sorrow and sighing will flee away (Isaiah 35:10).*

[10] *He saved them from the hand of the foe; from the hand of the enemy he redeemed them (Psalm 106:10).*

Sin is slavery. It can keep us bound like lonely prisoners. Eventually, it will kill us. But Jesus offers a ransom to deliver us. Not only does He buy us out of the captivity of greed, lust, and selfishness, but He also offers us rehabilitation. He offers us union with Him while we live on Earth, and perfect union with Him when we go to Heaven, where our names are written down in the Lamb's Book of Life.

You will one day dwell with God! How does that influence the way you will live today?

_____

_____

_____

MY NEW IDENTITY

Take time to study and contemplate the topics you have read. Which biblical image stood out to you? Pray these prayers. Allow God to meet with you as you rediscover who He has created you to be.

- Do you feel accepted in the family of God?

- Has your experience with marriage influenced how you interpret the "Bride of Christ" metaphor?

A prayer for those in the family of God who've wounded us: *Lord, forgive them. Like me, they've made mistakes. Remind them that as You parent them, You are good.*

A prayer for ourselves: *Lord, thank You for making me Your love. Even when human romantic relationships fail, You are always the love of my life. Help me see myself as You see me.*

Spend time in joyful worship, celebrating His acceptance, His desire for union with us. Celebrate today – no matter what else is occurring in your life. God is pursuing you!

CHAPTER SIX:

BODY of CHRIST

MANY EXPERIENCES AND conversations come to mind when I think about the Body of Christ. These days, so much talk is negative about the church and followers of Christ. I know why. We've all endured rejection, hypocrisy, rebellion, and terrible decisions. We've all contributed in some way.

But let's focus on the positive. We are all tiny portions of a larger body. Think of the Scripture we've read and studied already. Think back at the spiritual exercises you've practiced, the questions you've asked yourself, and the answers God has revealed to you. During this journey, realize this: God is changing you. He is renewing you. And even during painful portions of this process, you are already a key portion of the Body of Christ!

One of the experiences which helped me the most was praying with others.

In moments of desperation, we are more likely to seek prayer with others. That's what happened to me. I had been the one wanting to help people around me – soon I needed to be willing to receive the help from others. Though difficult initially, my life has never been the same.

An accident in December of 2007, and another in October of 2008, both injured my spine. The second fall actually bruised my spinal cord at the base of my skull; additionally, I ruptured a disk. The surgeon, hoping these injuries would heal, was slow to operate. What was I experiencing? Excruciating headaches. Mood swings. Unexpected feelings. Suicidal thoughts.

Being a man, I thought I could fight it off, but the intense pain kept pounding me. I couldn't sleep, and was in no condition to drive. One night I had to do something.

I called my church. A team of intercessors came and prayed over me. They prayed throughout the house. It was the last time I had those thoughts. Depression and suicidal thoughts left me. Though I just couldn't pray that day, I asked for the prayers of others. I **needed** the prayers of others. Everything changed.

What if I had not called them?

What if I had chosen isolation?

Living this life with a family of prayer partners moves us into a realm of healing and recovery. It helps us believe.

You are part of a large body. Call a small group, a church, a prayer line. Don't be bashful; don't be timid. Find someone to pray with you. It is crucial - it saved my life.

Refuse to live this life alone.

Live as the Body of Christ.

It helps us believe that change can occur.

It gives us hope!

BODY OF CHRIST

> [13] *For we were all baptized by one Spirit so as to form one body— whether Jews or Gentiles, slave or free—and we were all given the one Spirit to drink.* [14] *Even so the body is not made up of one part but of many (1 Corinthians 12:13-14).*

Jesus' death and resurrection make bodily resurrection of human beings possible (Rom. 6:5; 1 Cor. 15:3-26). It also makes their spiritual resurrection possible. "The Body of Christ" is the church, its limbs and organs made up of individual believers united and resurrected in Christ, working for shared gain (1 Cor. 12:12-31). Every person has a diverse gift to share, or a "part" to embrace, in the Body of believers that represent Jesus.

Are you doing your part in representing Christ on Earth?

_____

_____

_____

CHURCH OF GOD

To the church of God in Corinth, to those sanctified in Christ Jesus and called to be his holy people, together with all those everywhere who call on the name of our Lord Jesus Christ—their Lord and ours... (1 Corinthians 1:2).

As Christianity began to split off from the normal Jewish synagogue, the "Church of God" was clearly associated with Jesus Christ. He was its "head" (1 Cor. 12:12, 27; Rom. 12:4-5; Eph. 1:22-23; 4:15-16; Col. 1:18; 2:19), and believers its "body" (1 Cor. 12:12-31; Rom. 12:4-8). People joined through baptism in Christ's name (Rom. 6:3-4; Gal. 3:27) and shared life together in community. Some of these communities shared everything they had with each other.

JEWELS OF THE LORD

[17] "On the day when I act," says the LORD Almighty, "they will be my treasured possession. I will spare them, just as a father has compassion and spares his son who serves him" (Malachi 3:17).

It may be a cliché, but God made you individually unique, special. In spite of humanity's most sickly flaws, God still loves us and calls us His own. We're each made by Him and for Him. Malachi 3:17 refers to God's unique love for Israel. He chose them to be His people. He was fiercely partial to them. The same is true today of us. We, as Christians, are the new Israel. And He has set us apart as His treasure.

Are you living like you're God's treasure?

_____

_____

_____

MY NEW IDENTITY

Take time to study and contemplate the topics you have read. Which biblical image stood out to you? Consider the following questions and pray these prayers. Allow God to meet with you as you rediscover who He has created you to be within His body.

- What gifts has God given you?

- Are you guilty of being jealous of another person's role in the Body of Christ?

- Are there certain racial or cultural groups for which you harbor prejudice? Are you aware that they have a role to play, too?

A prayer for those who have discouraged our role in the Kingdom: *Lord, forgive them. Like me, they have made mistakes. Please remind them that we all have a part to play. Help us embrace healing and envision positive change.*

A prayer for ourselves: *Lord, thank You for making me unique, a part of Your body. Help me see myself as You see me.*

Spend time in joyful worship, celebrating His acceptance. Celebrate the Church today – no matter what else is occurring in your life. God has a part in His Kingdom for all of us. Join the celebration. Join in together.

CHAPTER SEVEN:

ROYAL PRIESTHOOD of CHRIST

OFTEN, WE ONLY think negative thoughts. The stories and Scripture shared throughout these pages have presented a different glance at life. We deal with our Identity correctly by seeing the many positives from God. How He sees us. What He says about us. Biblical truths which emphasize a new and true story about us.

Prior to my injuries and surgeries, I saw life in a positive way. I stayed in good shape. I played sports. Facing my physical problems and limitations, I could no longer be active in the same way.

How could I have a positive perspective while facing such painful realities of life? Rather than just facing my situation and pursuing God's peace, I initially kept thinking back. I traveled mentally in reverse – going through my teens again like I was walking down an alley picking up trash cans filled with all the garbage I had experienced.

I was living with regret. I was not realizing God had forgiven me of all my sins. I saw myself as a failure – my present physical weakness highlighted all the other weaknesses of my life journey.

A spiritual leader interrupted my mental and spiritual disaster. He spoke directly into my life, saying, "Jack, stop going down the alley and picking up the garbage can. Stop dwelling in the mess. You are a new creation."

His words were healing to me.

Christ had already picked up the garbage. I didn't need to pursue it and carry it. I was no longer that *old me*. I was new. I was new!

These passages of Scripture help me to continue hearing my friend's voice: "Jack, you've gotta stop! You are a new creature in Christ! You've gotta live like it!"

Please join me in listening to my friend's challenge. Please join me in reading, studying, meditating, memorizing, and believing these biblical truths.

We are adopted by God. We are the friends of God. We are blessed by God. We are the habitation of God. We are the Bride of Christ. We are the Body of Christ.

And, as we see in these verses, we are the Royal Priesthood of Christ. Think about those words: Royal…Priesthood…of Christ. Write them down. Repeat them. Believe them. Those words are about us – who we really are. Embrace them.

Stop seeing yourself through the lens of your weakness. Stop seeing yourself through the perspective of your mistakes. As the Royal Priesthood, listen with me to the words of my friend – put your name in place of mine:

"Jack, stop going down the alley and picking up the garbage can. Stop dwelling in the mess. You are a new creation."

"Jack, you've gotta stop! You are a new creature in Christ! You've gotta live like it!"

Read and believe with me the Words of our God.

ROYAL PRIESTHOOD

> [9] *But you are a chosen people, a royal priesthood, a holy nation, God's special possession, that you may declare the praises of him who called you out of darkness into his wonderful light (1 Peter 2:9).*

In the book of Hebrews, the author sets out to prove that the Christian faith is the completion and replacement of the patterns of worship seen in the Old Testament. Jesus, appointed by God, is the new High Priest (Heb. 5:5-10). Because of this, more than just an order of priests can have access to God's presence (Heb. 10:11-22). In fact, Christians are a new royal priesthood, one that is not dependent on a human family line. We no longer have to fear our God's judgment, but are invited to draw near, for we, too, are now righteous.

What kind of spiritual sacrifices have you had to make?

_____

_____

_____

CIRCUMCISION

³ For it is we who are the circumcision, we who serve God by his Spirit, who boast in Christ Jesus, and who put no confidence in the flesh... (Philippians 3:3).

In the Old Testament, circumcision was a sign of the covenant between God and the Hebrews. It set the Israelites apart from other cultures and signified promises made to Abraham. In the New Testament, after Jesus' message began to spread to the Gentiles, there was much debate on whether the practice should continue. Ultimately, without obedience and a changed heart, circumcision becomes un-circumcision (Rom. 2:25–29); the outward sign is irrelevant when compared with the realities of the heart. The Christian becoming a new creation internally (Gal. 6:15) was more important than stringent adherence to the external practices of the Old Law.

Are you following "the rules" to earn grace, or is your obedience birthed from a transformed heart?

MIGHTY

² Their children will be mighty in the land; the generation of the upright will be blessed (Psalm 112:2).

Because of frequent military skirmishes in Old Testament culture, Yahweh was often relied upon for His might. The God of Abraham, Isaac, and Jacob was a mighty God (Isa. 10:21), and He still is. With the ability to deliver, He is strong and yet still tender: "The Lord thy God in the midst of thee is mighty; He will save, He will rejoice over thee with joy; He will rest in his love, He will joy over thee with singing" (Zeph. 3:17).

What battles do you need help fighting?

_____

_____

_____

MY NEW IDENTITY

Take time to study and contemplate the topics you have read. Which biblical image stood out to you? Pray these prayers. Allow God to meet with you as you rediscover who He has created you to be.

- How does it feel to be a part of God's royal priesthood?

A prayer for those in need of God's might: *Lord, strengthen them. Remind them of Your victory on the cross.*

A prayer for ourselves: *Lord, thank You for making me part of Your holy priesthood. Set me apart. Help me see myself as You see me.*

Spend time in joyful worship, celebrating His acceptance, His fulfillment of the Law. Celebrate today – no matter what else is occurring in your life. God has ordained you for His work.

CHAPTER EIGHT:

PILLARS of TRUTH

WHAT IS TRUE? What will we believe? What thoughts, feelings, and beliefs control our moods and decisions? Is there a solid base of truth upon which we can depend?

The conflict is this: Are we going to believe what God says or what others say? Or, what we often say to ourselves in our thoughts and feelings?

We need to know the difference.

In each section of Identity Crisis, you can read the truth. Such truth often provides information much different from our initial thoughts. Yes, this is a crisis about our own Identity. And yes, through God's truth, we can begin to view life differently.

It happens when we grasp the pillars of truth.

I remember a simple conversation I had with Jack Frost. He said, "You and I will have the opportunity to listen to two voices: the Father of Creation or the father of lies. By pouring yourself into the Bible – the living Word of God – you will be able to discern the voice of the thoughts. You will know if those thoughts are from God or the enemy."

If the thoughts are from God, accept them.

If the thoughts are not from God, reject them.

God can guide us. We are the Pillars of Truth. We are to hold our thoughts captive to the obedience of Christ. He will direct our steps.

Here's a caution, though: don't try to go too fast. I've often walked right by God and missed what He had for me. I wasn't listening because I was in a hurry.

Learning to discern the truth is a maturing process that results in positive growth. Growth is a journey, not a destination.

Scripture can help us learn to slow down: Be still. Know that He is God. Even in the most trying moments of your life and see Jesus holding your hand as you walk with Him. He will get close to you – that is so important to remember. Grow in your relationship with Christ. Allow His Holy Spirit to change you.

It might not always feel good, but the outcome will always be good. Always. So, envision this. In doing so, you open your heart to Him and this becomes your prayer of intimacy.

- God is with you.

- Hold hands.

- Walk side by side.

- Envision that as you go for your prayer time – Jesus holding your hands and walking with you.

- Get close to Him.

- He will get close to you.

- He'll never give you more than you can handle.

- God is good all the time.

You: Adopted by God! You: Friend of God! You: Blessed by God! You: Habitation of God! You: Bride of Christ! You: Body of Christ! You: the Royal Priesthood of Christ!

You: Pillars of Truth!

Spiritual creatures, living stones: that is you!

PILLAR OF TRUTH

¹⁵ ...you will know how people ought to conduct themselves in God's household, which is the church of the living God, the pillar and foundation of the truth (1 Timothy 3:15).

Christ asserted that He was Truth personified (John 14:6; Eph. 4:21). The Holy Spirit can lead us to this Truth (John 16:13; 14:17; 1 John 4:6), in order for us to truly grasp it (John 8:32; 2 John 1), and demonstrate it (John 3:21). As members of Christ's church, or body, we have the immense responsibility of representing Truth in the world. It's our job to live out and testify to the teachings of Jesus. We can't do it perfectly on our own – but the Holy Spirit encourages us as we proclaim truth to those around us.

Has the Truth set you free?

_____

_____

_____

SPIRITUAL

¹ Brothers and sisters, if someone is caught in a sin, you who live by the Spirit should restore that person gently. But watch yourselves, or you also may be tempted (Galatians 6:1).

⁵ you also, like living stones, are being built into a spiritual house to be a holy priesthood, offering spiritual sacrifices acceptable to God through Jesus Christ (1 Peter 2:5).

We are not just physical beings. God created us with unseen aspects (Gen. 1:27a). Everyone has a spirit, and everyone is spiritual. But those who seek after the Spirit of Truth listen to the Holy Spirit and manifest the Fruit of the Spirit: love, joy, peace, patience, gentleness, goodness, faithfulness, kindness, and self-control.

Are you cultivating the Fruit of the Spirit?

_____

_____

_____

LIVING STONES

> [4] *As you come to him, the living Stone—rejected by humans but chosen by God and precious to him—* [5] *you also, like living stones, are being built into a spiritual house to be a holy priesthood, offering spiritual sacrifices acceptable to God through Jesus Christ (1 Peter 2:4-5).*

In 1 Peter 2:4-5, the author emphasizes the significance of Christian kinship. Sometimes, in our extremely individualistic society, we forget that we're working together to build "a spiritual house." God now inhabits more than just an Old Testament temple. By the Holy Spirit, He lives with and within His people. And while we do come to resurrected life in Christ individually (1 Pet. 1:23; see 2:2), we are not little islands unto ourselves – we're building blocks for a "spiritual temple" (2:5).

MY NEW IDENTITY

Take time to study and contemplate the topics you have read. Which biblical image stood out to you? Consider the following questions and pray these prayers. Allow God to meet with you as you rediscover who He has created you to be.

• Are there any truths difficult for you to accept?

A prayer for the friends who ignore the truth: *Lord, forgive them. Like me, they have made mistakes. Please reveal to them Your love and right standing with You.*

A prayer for ourselves: *Lord, thank You for being the Way, the Truth, and the Life. Help me to embrace Your truth. Help me see myself as You see me.*

Spend time in joyful worship, celebrating His acceptance, His Truth. Celebrate today – no matter what else is occurring in your life. God has shown you the truth!

CHAPTER NINE:

TREASURE of GOD

I T WAS 30 degrees at 4:30 am. My father had gone outside in the snow and ice to smoke.

He fell and broke his hip.

He lay there for 45 minutes.

I believe it was the Spirit of God who woke me up. I knew something was wrong.

I went outside and walked directly to my dad. It was amazing how God had protected him. I wrapped him in blankets and called 911.

My father was 88 years old at the time. He needed a hip replaced. The health care professionals worked him hard – he eventually got out of the nursing home. But every day for four months, he had physical therapy. They massaged his hips, pushed him to walk and exercise. They worked to make him stronger.

Now 90, he walks with a walker but is getting around okay.

If he had not worked through the recovery process, he would not have improved. If he refused to walk – even using the walker – he would not be improving.

He needed to view himself as a rescued treasure – a rescued treasure to be nurtured and strengthened.

Have your injuries hindered your growth and development? Have you fallen and struggled to work through your season of recovery?

Today, view yourself as God's Treasure. You are no accident.

Read and study about being the Treasure of God. Meditate on the wonderful opportunity of obeying God rather than being deceived by fears or doubts or hate or hurts. Realize you are God's beloved.

Today is your day for a new Identity!

TREASURE OF GOD

> *⁴ For the LORD has chosen Jacob to be his own, Israel to be his treasured possession (Psalm 135:4).*

Were you ever picked last in gym class? Passed over for a job promotion? We've all felt, at some point, that we're just not good enough. But God sees us differently. He sees us as cherished children. He chooses us—not because we're perfect and holy, but because He is. In the Old Testament, Israel was God's chosen people. In this New Testament age, all who accept Christ are welcomed into His Kingdom.

Knowing that God accepts you, is the pain of rejection from man as strong?

_____

_____

_____

OBEDIENT

> *¹⁴ As obedient children, do not conform to the evil desires you had when you lived in ignorance (1 Peter 1:14).*

The Greek word for obedience, "*hupotasso*" is actually a military term, meaning "to rank under." God is the supreme authority, all-powerful and above everything on Earth. But while the term obedience may have a military connotation, it does not mean God is a red-faced drill sergeant!

We can trust His commands because we know He *loves* us and wants to protect His treasure. We can obey His ways because they will keep us from harm (Ps. 19:7-8).

Is there an area in which you are struggling to obey God?

_____

_____

_____

BELOVED OF GOD

> *⁴ But for those who fear you, you have raised a banner to be unfurled against the bow. ⁵Save us and help us with your right hand, that those you love may be delivered (Psalm 60:4-5).*
>
> *⁵ Be exalted, O God, above the heavens; let your glory be over all the earth.*
> *⁶ Save us and help us with your right hand, that those you love may be delivered (Psalm 108:5-6).*

God's love is personal. It's even deeper than that of a mother for her children (Is. 49:15; 66:13). Love is part of God's personality. It is not dependent on our performance or disobedience. We are beloved of God with an "everlasting" love (Jer. 31:3). Jesus revealed this love by His countless acts of compassionate healing (Mark 1:41; Luke 7:13), His teaching about God's acceptance of the sinner (Luke 15:11ff; 18:10ff.). The whole drama of redemption, centering as it does on the death of Christ, is divine love in action!

Is it hard for you to accept that you're beloved of God?

_____

_____

_____

MY NEW IDENTITY

Take time to study and contemplate the topics you have read. Which biblical image stood out to you? Consider the following questions and pray these prayers. Allow God to meet with you as you rediscover who He has created you to be.

- Are you treating others as if they're beloved by God?

A prayer for those who have encouraged our disobedience: *Lord, forgive them. Like me, they've made mistakes. Remind them of Your mercy.*

A prayer for ourselves: *Lord, thank You for making me Your treasure. Help me to trust and obey You. Help me see myself as You see me.*

Spend time in joyful worship, celebrating His loving laws. Celebrate today – no matter what else is occurring in your life. God has made you His treasure!

CHAPTER TEN:

VESSELS of MERCY

I'VE TOLD YOU about my Dad. Things have been tough, yes. But it is an honor to take care of my father. When I help him, when I ask him questions, when I try to understand what he's thinking, I learn so much from this 90 year old man.

He needs mercy. I realize how much I need the mercy of my Heavenly Father, too. I also realize how we are all called to be God's Vessels of Mercy.

I was a regional sales manager. The job was a *dream-come-true* for me. Then, in the middle of the recession, I fell, injuring my spine. Now unable to work, I couldn't sell the house. I lost everything – all of the material things, anyway.

I began living with my father. My financial situation continued to grow worse. One part of me was thinking, "What are you going to do with such little money?"

Over the years, God has taught me much about trusting Him. Uplifted by these Scriptural truths, I knew I couldn't give up. I couldn't let the doubt control my mood.

I began to talk back: "It is not my problem. God is big enough to handle this."

He will give me the wisdom I need to respond wisely. I believed that even when I didn't feel like it. I had spent years tithing and giving. A large percentage of my money had gone to missionaries and feeding the poor.

Suddenly a check came in the mail. Workers' compensation started paying. God reminded me of how my Father in heaven takes care of me in the same way that I had been taking care of my earthly father. I had this steadfast faith that I did not need to worry about how my bills would be paid. God said He would open up the windows of heaven and bless me.

Would I receive His words? Would I believe Him?

Now I get to know my father better than I knew him during my childhood because of my rebellion and leaving home early. We do things together. We eat together and go to movies.

Though I am on full disability through the severity of my injuries, I am believing God is going to heal my soul and my body. Though I am still living in need of a miracle, I stand upon God's mercy. Those words describe my life now.

Can you let them describe your life? Whatever situation you are facing, can you write the words God's Mercy over every aspect of your life?

VESSELS OF MERCY

23 What if he did this to make the riches of his glory known to the objects of his mercy, whom he prepared in advance for glory... (Romans 9:23).

7 Blessed are the merciful, for they will be shown mercy (Matthew 5:7).

God's ultimate sign of mercy toward humanity was in sending Jesus to us (Luke 1:58; Eph. 2:4; Rom. 11:30-32). We deserved death but were given eternal life! We've been presented the ultimate pardon – so how is it that we cannot pardon those who have offended *us*? Jesus, in the Sermon on the Mount, urges us to forgive "our debtors" (Matt. 5:12).

Because God showed us mercy and forgiveness in Jesus, we have no option but to be merciful and forgiving in our daily lives.

Is there someone in your life that you need to pardon?

_____

_____

_____

BRETHREN

[1] Therefore, I urge you, brothers and sisters, in view of God's mercy, to offer your bodies as a living sacrifice, holy and pleasing to God— this is your true and proper worship (Romans 12:1).

[29] For those God foreknew he also predestined to be conformed to the image of his Son, that he might be the firstborn among many brothers and sisters (Romans 8:29).

When we're reborn into the family of God, we suddenly get lots of brothers and sisters! Just like with any family, siblings can fight and show favoritism. But in light of the way God has treated us, we must try to show the same kind of love to everyone around us. God has been incredibly merciful, so we must show mercy, sacrificing our need for superiority. True worship isn't just singing songs with a crowd in church – it's also treating those people, your spiritual siblings with respect.

Do you owe a brother or sister in Christ an apology?

_____

_____

_____

MY NEW IDENTITY

Take time to study and contemplate the topics you have read. Which Biblical image stood out to you? Consider the following questions and pray these prayers. Allow God to meet with you as you rediscover His view of you.

- To whom do you need to show mercy?

- Has anyone ever shown you mercy in a time of need?

A prayer for the people who have failed to show us mercy: *Lord, forgive them. Like me, they have made mistakes. Please remind them of Your mercy. Help me to let go of the past.*

A prayer for ourselves: *Lord, thank you for being merciful to me. Help me show mercy to others. Help me see myself as You see me – nothing more, nothing less.*

Spend time in joyful worship, celebrating His acceptance, His mercy. Celebrate today – no matter what else is occurring in your life. God has been merciful to you.

CHAPTER ELEVEN:

LIGHT of the WORLD

R EADING THESE VERSES, studying the topical meanings, and writing these stories reminded me that *even I* can help others. Yes, I can. I can!

In the past, I thought that just the people who seem to have it all together would be the ones strong and wise enough to help others. Or, I thought that just the people who appear to have everything go their way were people of enough value to help others.

I was wrong. I realize now that I am valuable to God.

Me! Yes, me! Even I can help others!

And by helping others, I can made a difference in my community and in our world.

Making a difference in our culture – that's what following Christ is all about. When I speak to people about Christ's love, I am not just talking to them through the excitement of my early days of following Christ. I am not just speaking with enthusiasm.

I write and speak through experience. Experience of wounds, of scars, of fears, of doubts. Experience of finding faith in the middle of life's storms.

What's the result? When God carries us through the painful life experiences, what might happen?

Jesus described it as shining like light in a dark world.

What happens to darkness when light appears? Darkness leaves. The light shines.

That is what I can do. That is what you can do.

Christ in us – we are the light shining so brightly that the word's darkness has no chance.

So, where does it start? In realizing the realities of the titles you've studied through these pages. These descriptions have reworked your thinking. Your Identity Crisis has moved from thoughts of darkness to an awareness of the now being the Light of the World!

God views you that way.

Choose to view yourself that way.

Read each word. Believe each word. Receive each word.

Be faithful. Be fruitful.

Welcome your new Identity.

And wave goodbye to the darkness.

LIGHT OF THE WORLD

14 You are the light of the world. A town built on a hill cannot be hidden (Matthew 5:14).

The first thing God created was light (Gen. 1:3). As if with a garment, He is clothed in it (Ps. 104:2), and night is not dark to him (Ps. 139:12). In the book of Revelation, God is described as the light of His servants (Rev. 22:5). Christ considers Himself "the light of the world" (John 8:12; 9:5), and He gives this light to His followers to carry (Matt. 5:14). Do you remember the song, "This Little Light of Mine"? Although it may be a children's song, the message is significant. Do we hide Christ's light under a "bushel" of insecurity or fear? Or do we let His love illuminate out from us?

Are you scared of what you'll see when Christ's light shines on you?

_____

_____

_____

FAITHFUL

¹ Paul, an apostle of Christ Jesus by the will of God, to God's holy people in Ephesus, the faithful in Christ Jesus... (Ephesians 1:1).

² To God's holy people in Colossae, the faithful brothers and sisters in Christ: Grace and peace to you from God our Father (Colossians 1:2).

Faithful can have two connotations: being full of faith, or having steadfast commitment. Both aspects are necessary for the Christian life. The followers of God are sometimes collectively called "The Faithful" in Scripture. They're responsible for shining God's light in the world, bearing fruit for God's kingdom, until He returns.

Are you fully committed to Christ?

_____

_____

_____

FRUITFUL

¹⁰ ...so that you may live a life worthy of the Lord and please him in every way: bearing fruit in every good work, growing in the knowledge of God...(Colossians 1:10).

Depending on the soil it grows in and the amount of water and sunlight it receives, fruit can taste sweet or bitter. The same concept is true of our "spiritual fruit." If we surround ourselves with toxins and darkness, our fruit is going to wither and die, and possibly kill others in the process!

Do you need some spiritual weed-killer?

_____

_____

_____

MY NEW IDENTITY

Take time to study and contemplate the topics you have read. Which biblical image stood out to you? Consider the following questions and pray these prayers. Allow God to meet with you as you rediscover who He has created you to be: light in the world.

- What keeps you from shining more brightly?

A prayer for ourselves: *Lord, thank You for illuminating our lives with Your Spirit. Help me to see myself as You see me.*

Spend time in joyful worship, celebrating His acceptance, His Light. Celebrate today – no matter what else is occurring in your life for God shines His light on you!

CHAPTER TWELVE

WATCHMEN of GOD

N ow. Now is the time. In the final portion of this book, join me and believe this: Now is the time for you to receive your new Identity.

It helps to once again think about *who we have been* in the past and *who God wants us to be* in the present and the future. Let's go there one more time.

Ask yourself some questions like these:

Can you make a difference? What about your Identity? How have these words changed your thought process about who you are, about what you can do, and about the impact you can have on our culture?

Do you believe you are adopted by God? Do you believe today – yes, at this very moment – you are a friend of God?

Has God blessed you? How? When? What have you done with His blessings?

Are you now seeing yourself as the habitation of God?

Are you now seeing yourself as the Bride of Christ?

Are you now – yes, at this very moment – seeing yourself as the Royal Priesthood of Christ?

Any thoughts about these phrases: Pillars of Truth? Treasure of God? Vessels of Mercy? Light of the World?

As you process thoughts regarding this new Identity, we want to end by giving you this name: The Watchmen of God.

Read these passages. Once again, think about you. Think of how you are a NEW YOU. The old is gone. The new is alive and well.

You will never be the same.

And because you are part of God's plan to bring change throughout the world, the lives of many others will never be the same.

Get ready. His Kingdom is coming. His will is being done.

In you!

WATCHMAN

8 Listen! Your watchmen lift up their voices; together they shout for joy. When the LORD returns to Zion, they will see it with their own eyes (Isaiah 52:8).

6 I have posted watchmen on your walls, Jerusalem; they will never be silent day or night. You who call on the LORD, give yourselves no rest... (Isaiah 62:6).

In biblical times, watchtowers were erected for two purposes: 1) To guard livestock or wine vineyards from wild animals and thieves (2 Ch. 26:10; Mic. 4:8; Isa. 27:3). 2) In larger cities, watchtowers were strongholds of military defense. Watchmen practiced constant vigilance, for it was their duty to alert the city and the King in the event of invasion (2 Sam. 18:24-27; 2 Kings 9:17-20). Nighttime was the most dangerous time for these guards, so they were always fervently waiting for the sunrise.

As Christians today, we are charged with being watchmen for the church. We guard our brothers and sisters in Christ from false teaching, poor choices, and traps the Devil might set. We eagerly await Jesus' return.

Are you on alert?

_____

_____

_____

FLOCK OF GOD

28 Keep watch over yourselves and all the flock of which the Holy Spirit has made you overseers. Be shepherds of the church of God, which he bought with his own blood (Acts 20:28).

3 The gatekeeper opens the gate for him, and the sheep listen to his voice. He calls his own sheep by name and leads them out. 4 When he has brought out all his own, he goes on ahead of them, and his sheep follow him because they know his voice (John 10:3-4).

16 Again Jesus said, "Simon son of John, do you love me?" He answered, "Yes, Lord, you know that I love you." Jesus said, "Take care of my sheep" (John 21:16).

16 I have other sheep that are not of this sheep pen. I must bring them also. They too will listen to my voice, and there shall be one flock and one shepherd (John 10:16).

In the Gospels, Jesus often used a shepherding metaphor to describe His relationship with His followers. Jesus is the good shepherd. He's willing to lay his life down for His flock. Those who follow Him are His sheep. We're forever protected and guided by His voice (John 10:4), which helps us steer clear of the wolves.

Are you recognizing the Shepherd's voice in your daily life?

_____

_____

_____

MY NEW IDENTITY

Take time to study and contemplate the topics you have read. Which biblical image stood out to you? Consider the following questions and pray these prayers. Allow God to meet with you as you rediscover who He has created you to be: a Watchman of God.

- Who has God put in your life for you to watch over?

- Do you have anyone older and wiser watching over you?

A prayer for those who have failed to watch over us: *Lord, forgive them. Like me, they have made mistakes. Please remind them that they have been positioned by You to protect those under their care.*

A prayer for ourselves: *Lord, thank You for watching over me. Help me to guide others in their faith. Help me to see myself as You do.*

Spend time in joyful worship, celebrating His acceptance, His protection. Celebrate today!

CHAPTER THIRTEEN:

LOVED by GOD

CHAPTER TWELVE APPEARED to conclude Identity Crisis. What more can we add? What other topics, themes, words, and passages of Scripture remind us of who we are in Christ? What other phrase can redirect our thoughts into biblical correctness?

The words reminded you of this: Now is the time for your new Identity. By believing in your adoption by God, by believing in a friendship with God, by believing that you are made new, you have dealt properly with an Identity Crisis.

You haven't given up. You haven't quit. You haven't tried to conquer this crisis on your own. You've decided to welcome the will of the Father. You've chosen to wave goodbye to the old. You've stepped into the path of righteousness – and you're letting this journey guide you from glory to glory.

You will never be the same, right?

And since you'll never be the same, what is one more word to describe this NEW YOU? As we glance through Scripture and seek to grasp a new Identity, can the many verses be summarized with one word? A word reflecting the life of Christ. A word revealing the reality of our new Identity. A word which should be the vision of each church, the goal of each family, the true purpose of each of us.

The word is love.

God reminded me of His love when He woke me up from my sleep of worthlessness. He woke me up and said, "You are my son. I love you.

I will never leave you. I accept you. I enjoy my time with you. There is nothing you can do to stop Me from loving you."

Join me, today. Wake up and know you are God's child. Stand up and begin a new walk into glory with your mind focused on this truth: GOD LOVES YOU.

Freedom comes from knowing about being adopted into the Kingdom family. Sonship. That's what I like to call it. Adopted by God. In the family. THE family. Sonship.

Grasping His love moves us into a realm of reality that is rare in our culture, our churches, and our self examinations. God's love says, "You do not need to perform."

So many of us as Christians think we need to perform for God. Before we knew Christ, our lives lacked this true love. But often, even after our salvation, we feel like little kids needing to perform to earn love from our Heavenly Father.

Performance has always been a big thing in my life. I've carried it into my relationship with God, believing somehow that if I perform better, I could earn love from Him.

That had to change. I received the revelation:

- of being a son,

- of waking up a son,

- of going to bed a son,

- of being in sonship with my Creator.

His love is so freeing!

That must also change for you. Today. In whatever else you are experiencing and enduring. Regardless of what other lies you've been told – at home, in church, in our own mind, through relationships, through mistakes you've made, by fear, by hate, by wounds.

Today is the day for love. Say goodbye to performance and hello to God's love. Today!

Receive the revelation:

- of being a son/daughter,

- of waking up a son/daughter,

- of going to bed a son/daughter,

- of being in sonship with our Creator!

His love is so freeing for YOU!

His love sets YOU free!

The truth of divine, pure, eternal love sets YOU free!

So many times, we go on our feelings. That is okay as long as our feelings are based on truth. If we believe a lie, then we think a lie and feel a lie and live a lie. But now we are believing the truth of love.

If we have our mind renewed by the truth, our belief system becomes renewed based on truth rather than

- lies

- deception

- performance

- pain

- rejection

- worthlessness

- defilement

- insecurity

- abuse

- misunderstanding

- feelings

- hurts

- wounds

- scars

- desires

- fears

- hopelessness

- shame

We must no longer think the way we once thought – we realize we don't need to perform for God. Do you still ask yourself those questions: What can I do to make Him happy? What can I do to make Him love me? To finally love me? To convince Him to answer my prayers and work for the good in my life?

The fact of the matter is this: we've all been given a measurable amount of faith. That action of faith meets God's grace – God's undeserved favor.

Each page of this book can be summarized with this chapter's theme: Love.

I pray that each page of your life will be summarized by that same theme: Love.

PRECIOUS

> *⁸ But God demonstrates his own love for us in this: While we were still sinners, Christ died for us (Romans 5:8).*
>
> *⁵ And hope does not put us to shame, because God's love has been poured out into our hearts through the Holy Spirit, who has been given to us (Romans 5:5).*
>
> *⁷ How priceless is your unfailing love, O God! People take refuge in the shadow of your wings (Psalm 36:7).*

Our human relationships can sometimes blur the way we view God and His love for us. Maybe your siblings were favored over you. Maybe you don't feel you have skills or talents that make you "special." When those we trust mistreat us, it can cause us to second-guess our standing with the Lord. But as Romans 5:8 says, God loved us enough to send His Son to die for us. *Because of His great love for us, God, who is rich in mercy made us alive with Christ even when we were dead in transgressions—it is by grace you have been saved (Ephesians 2:4-5).* He cares enough to bring each of us into His kingdom, a place where we are not just tolerated – we are chosen.

FOLD OF GOD

> *¹⁰ Be devoted to one another in love. Honor one another above yourselves (Romans 12:10).*
>
> *⁷ Dear friends, let us love one another, for love comes from God. Everyone who loves has been born of God and knows God.⁸ Whoever does not love does not know God, because God is love (1 John 4:7-8).*
>
> *¹⁰ Love does no harm to a neighbor. Therefore love is the fulfillment of the law (Romans 13:10).*

¹⁵ I no longer call you servants, because a servant does not know his master's business. Instead, I have called you friends, for everything that I learned from my Father I have made known to you (John 15:15).

⁸ Above all, love each other deeply, because love covers over a multitude of sins (1 Peter 4:8).

We can experience God in several ways, but one of the most tangible is in Christian community. The term "fold of God" is similar to "flock of God." In fact, "fold" refers to a "sheepfold," which is a safe, secure place where a flock of sheep would rest together. When we accept Jesus, we can enter into a community that embodies Him in our everyday lives. We can seek Him together as well as on our own *I love those who love me, and those who seek me find me (Proverbs 8:17).* While no church will ever be perfect, it is the goal to offer a safe place to receive discipline *because the LORD disciplines those he loves (Proverbs 3:12),* and Christ-like love.

HEAVEN

¹⁶ For God so loved the world that he gave his one and only Son, that whoever believes in him shall not perish but have eternal life (John 3:16).

³⁷ No, in all these things we are more than conquerors through him who loved us. ³⁸ For I am convinced that neither death nor life, neither angels nor demons, neither the present nor the future, nor any powers, ³⁹ neither height nor depth, nor anything else in all creation, will be able to separate us from the love of God that is in Christ Jesus our Lord (Romans 8:37-39).

³⁵ Who shall separate us from the love of Christ? Shall trouble or hardship or persecution or famine or nakedness or danger or sword? (Romans 8:35)

The subject of Heaven has always been surrounded by controversy and debate. What will it look like? Will we go there immediately after death? Regardless of our views on its exact physicality and location, this much is clear: God will be there. We will finally meet Him face to face and sorrows from this world will pass away. The precious fold of God will continue to be His even after this life ends. But we shouldn't wait until then to enjoy His presence! Even in the hardest of struggles, God's love is there to comfort us, to bring us the treasures of Heaven on Earth.

MY NEW IDENTITY

Take time to study and contemplate the topics you have read. Which biblical image stood out to you? Consider the following questions and pray these prayers. Allow God to meet with you as you rediscover who He has created you to be, in light of who He is.

- What makes you feel unworthy of God's love?

- Are you willing to turn that pain over to God?

- How do you personally show God that you love Him?

- In what situations do you feel God's love strongly?

- Is your view of love accurate? Contemplate on 1 Corinthians 13:

¹ If I speak in the tongues of men or of angels, but do not have love, I am only a resounding gong or a clanging cymbal.² If I have the gift of prophecy and can fathom all mysteries and all knowledge, and if I have a faith that can move mountains, but do not have love, I am nothing.³ If I give all I possess to the poor and give over my body to hardship that I may boast, but do not have love, I gain nothing.⁴ Love is patient, love is kind. It does not envy, it does not boast, it is not proud.⁵ It does not dishonor others, it is not self-seeking, it is not easily angered, it keeps no record of wrongs.⁶ Love does not delight in evil but rejoices with the truth.⁷ It always protects, always trusts, always hopes, always perseveres.⁸ Love never fails. But where there are prophecies, they will cease; where there are tongues, they will be stilled; where there is knowledge, it will pass away.⁹ For we know in part and we prophesy in part,¹⁰ but when completeness comes, what is in part disappears.¹¹ When I was a child, I talked like a child, I thought like a child, I reasoned like a child. When I became a man, I put the ways of childhood behind me.¹² For now we see only a reflection as in a mirror; then we shall see face to face. Now I know in part; then I shall know fully, even as I am fully known.¹³ And now these three remain: faith, hope and love. But the greatest of these is love (1 Corinthians 13).

A prayer for those who've failed to love us: *Father, forgive them. Like me, they have made mistakes. As Your word says, help me to pray for my enemies and love those who antagonize me. But I tell you, love your enemies and pray for those who persecute you, (Matthew 5:44).*

A prayer for ourselves: *Father, thank You for loving me. I don't deserve it. Help me see myself as You see me - nothing more, nothing less. As 1 Corinthians 16:14 says, help me to do everything in love.*

Spend time in joyful worship, celebrating His acceptance, His unfailing love. Celebrate by giving that kind of love to others. Memorize the following verse:

³⁴ A new command I give you: Love one another. As I have loved you, so you must love one another.³⁵ By this everyone will know that you are my disciples, if you love one another" (John 13:34-35).

CHAPTER FOURTEEN:

DISPELLING LIES

Yes, I am a convicted felon. Yes, I've been hooked on narcotic drugs. Yes, I've spent countless nights awake suffering from withdrawal. Yes, you have read right through these pages about my hurts, my weaknesses, my scars, and my failures. Yes, I've made some poor decisions. Yes, health problems have hindered me.

But the promises and declarations which have covered these pages have invaded my heart. I'm not only a convicted felon – I am a forgiven son of God. I not only know about hurts and failures – I know about healing and redemption. Even when in pain and in moments of uncertainty, I personally know the God who heals, who forgives, and who restores.

Do you know Him?

There is more to my life story than my mistakes. There is victory and hope. There is forgiveness and a future.

No matter what you are experiencing today, you can know Him. Last year, I learned even more about knowing Him in a deeper way. After surgery in January 2011, I knew my life needed to change once again. I had become highly addicted to pain medication.

In June 2011, I felt myself spiraling downward. We put my Dad in a nursing home and I checked myself into The Caron Foundation for a season of drug rehabilitation. After 32 days, I placed myself in an extensive spinal cord rehabilitation for ten weeks. I was facing so many problems at once. But though my spine and the rest of my body struggled, the presence of God was with me. He met me there. I just needed faith to believe that His grace had met me. That's why I can now be living exceeding above my wildest imagination.

I got my life back. Let me give an example of that. After my release from the rehabilitation center, I started going back to the gym. I started doing what I used to love and do on a regular basis. I began lifting weights again. Can you imagine that? I had the strength, the health, and the wholeness needed to start taking good care of myself again. I was clear-headed and right-minded, and it felt like I was back in charge of my own choices. I felt His favor, His purpose, and His help to get back engaged with all sorts of positive pursuits.

I want you to get your life back, too!

Realize it is all about Jesus. He has done the work. He gave me the courage to push through. Let Him do that for you.

This wonderful Jesus is for all of us – for you and for me and for all who will say yes to His invitation to change their identity.

Tap into this life. Tap into this gospel. It takes faith and discipline, sure. But it is a free gift from a loving Father. Let us never resist it.

The following verses replace the lies with truth. The words you read, pray, study, and think have the power to change your self-view into a new, God-directed identity.

Your identity crisis has met you. But your God has met your identity crisis. He has spoken. He has spoken words of life, words of truth, words of redemption, and words of freedom.

His Word dispels the lies. The deception from years of false beliefs is now replaced with this reality: YOU HAVE A NEW IDENTITY.

Slowly read and meditate on these declarations. Believe them. When you doubt, choose to not let the feelings control your decision to accept what God is saying to you.

THE TRUTH ABOUT INSECURITY
"I'm safe in the arms of my Father"

1. I am surrounded by my Father

Just as Jerusalem is protected by mountains on every side, the Lord protects his people by holding them in his arms now and forever. (Psalm 125:2; Contemporary English Version)

2. My Father holds me tenderly close to Him.

He tends his flock like a shepherd: He gathers them close to his heart. (Isaiah 40:11a)

3. I am tucked away and safe.

He will cover you with his feathers, and under his wings you will find refuge; his faithfulness will be your shield and rampart. (Psalm 91:4)

4. I am hidden in my Father.

You are my hiding place; you will protect me from trouble and surround me with songs of deliverance. (Psalm 32:7)

For you died and your life is now hidden with Christ in God. (Colossians 3:3)

For in the day of trouble he will keep me safe in his dwelling; he will hide me in the shelter of his tabernacle and set me high upon a rock. (Psalm 27:5)

5. I am encompassed by my Father's love.

The Lord's unfailing love surrounds the man who trusts in him. (Psalm 32:10b)

6. My Father is with me, regardless of what is happening around me.

When you pass through the waters, I will be with you; and when you pass through the rivers, they will not sweep over you. When you walk through the fire, you will not be burned; the flames will not set you ablaze. (Isaiah 43:2)

7. My Father is continually available to help me.

So we say with confidence, "The Lord is my helper; I will not be afraid. What can man do to me?" (Hebrews 13:6)

8. My Father is with me and will never leave me.

The Lord himself goes before you and will be with you; he will never leave you nor forsake you. Do not be afraid; do not be discouraged. (Deuteronomy 31:8)

9. My Father is in control of my life.

But I trust in you O LORD; I say, "You are my God." My times are in your hands. (Psalm 31:14,15a)

10. My Father has given me a place of security to stand in.

He lifted me out of the slimy pit, out of the mud and the mire; he set my feet on a rock and gave me a firm place to stand. (Psalm 40:2)

11. His Fatherly eyes watch over me and His loving heart has already planned help for me.

Cast all your anxiety on him because he cares for you. (1 Peter 5:7)

THE TRUTH ABOUT FEAR

"I am not alone. The Father is with me."

1. My Father is always with me. He will never leave me.

   "...And surely I am with you always, to the very end of the age."
   (Matthew 28:20b)

   The LORD replied, "My Presence will go with you, and I will give
   you rest." (Exodus 33:14)

   When you pass through the waters, I will be with you; and through
   the rivers, they will not overflow you. When you walk through the
   fire, you will not be scorched, nor will the flame burn you. (Isaiah
   43:2, New American Standard Bible)

2. My Father wants to hold and comfort me when I'm afraid.

   For thus says the LORD, "Behold, I extend peace to her like a river,
   and the glory of the nations like an overflowing stream; and you will
   be nursed, you will be carried on the hip and fondled on the knees. As
   one whom his mother comforts, so I will comfort you; and you will be
   comforted in Jerusalem." (Isaiah 66:12-13, New American Standard
   Bible)

3. My Father is lovingly and faithfully watching over me.

   He will not let your foot slip—he who watches over you will not
   slumber; indeed, he who watches over Israel will neither slumber
   nor sleep. The LORD will watch over your life. The LORD will
   watch over your coming and going both now and forevermore. (Psalm
   121:3,4,7,8)

4. My Father has confidence in me. (He provides all that I
   need in every situation.)

I can do everything through him who gives me strength. (Philippians 4:13)

5. The Father is always present to help me.

The LORD is my strength and my shield; my heart trusts in him, and I am helped. My heart leaps for joy and I will give thanks to him in song. (Psalm 28:7)

So do not fear, for I am with you; do not be dismayed, for I am your God. I will strengthen you and help you; I will uphold you with my righteous right hand. (Isaiah 41:10)

It is the Sovereign LORD who helps me. Who is he that will condemn me? They will all wear out like a garment; the moths will eat them up. (Isaiah 50:9)

So we say with confidence, "The Lord is my helper; I will not be afraid. What can man do to me?" (Hebrews 13:6)

6. I can rest in the strong and capable arms of my Father.

The eternal God is your refuge, and underneath are the everlasting arms. He will drive out your enemy before you, saying, "Destroy them!" (Deuteronomy 33:27)

Even to your old age and gray hairs I am he, I am he who will sustain you. I have made you and I will carry you; I will sustain you and I will rescue you. (Isaiah 46:4)

7. My Father is always there for me. He wants me to trust Him.

Don't let your hearts be troubled. Trust in God, and trust also in me. (John 14:1, New Living Translation)

May the God of hope fill you with all joy and peace as you trust in him, so that you may overflow with hope by the power of the Holy Spirit. (Romans 15:13)

But I trust in your unfailing love; my heart rejoices in your salvation. (Psalm 13:5)

When I am afraid, I will trust in you. In God, whose word I praise, in God I trust; I will not be afraid. What can mortal man do to me? (Psalm 56:3-4)

Trust in the LORD with all your heart and lean not on your own understanding; in all your ways acknowledge him, and he will make your paths straight. (Proverbs 3:5-6)

THE TRUTH ABOUT REJECTION

"I am accepted by my Father."

1. I am chosen, treasured, and loved.

You did not choose me, but I choose you... (John 15:16a)

Therefore, as God's chosen people, holy and dearly loved, clothe yourselves with compassion, kindness, humility, gentleness and patience. Bear with each other and forgive whatever grievances you may have against one another. Forgive as the Lord forgave you. (Colossians 3:12-13)

For you are a people holy to the LORD your God. The LORD your God has chosen you out of all the peoples on the face of the earth to be his people, his treasured possession. (Deuteronomy 7:6)

But now, this is what the LORD says—he who created you, O Jacob, he who formed you, O Israel: "Fear not, for I have redeemed you; I have summoned you by name; you are mine." (Isaiah 43:1)

2. I belong to the Father.

Do you not know that your body is a temple of the Holy Spirit, who is in you, whom you have received from God? You are not your own; you were bought at a price. Therefore honor God with your body. (1 Corinthians 6:19-20)

3. I am a child of the Father.

Yet to all who received him, to those who believed in his name, he gave the right to become children of God. (John 1:12)

4. I am Christ's friend.

I no longer call you servants, because a servant does not know his master's business. Instead, I have called you friends, for everything that I learned from my Father I have made known to you. (John 15:15)

5. I am a member of Christ's family.

Now you are the body of Christ, and each one of you is a part of it. (1 Corinthians 12:27)

6. The Father loves me so much that He adopted me.

For he chose us in him before the creation of the world to be holy and blameless in his sight. In love he predestined us to be adopted as his sons through Jesus Christ, in accordance with his pleasure and will to the praise of his glorious grace, which he has freely given us in the One he loves. (Ephesians 1:4-7)

7. My Father is always for me, never against me.

What, then, shall we say in response to this? If God is for us, who can be against us? (Romans 8:31)

8. My Father will never forget me. I have always been loved by Him.

Can a mother forget the baby at her breast and have no compassion on the child she has borne? Though she may forget, I will not forget you! See, I have engraved you on the palms of my hands; your walls are ever before me. (Isaiah 49:15-16)

The LORD appeared to us in the past, saying: "I have loved you with an everlasting love; I have drawn you with loving-kindness." (Jeremiah 31:3)

9. Troubles do not separate me from the Father's love.

Who shall separate us from the love of Christ? Shall trouble or hardship or persecution or famine or nakedness or danger or sword? As it is written: "For your sake we face death all day long; we are considered as sheep to be slaughtered." No, in all these things we are more than conquerors through him who loved us. For I am convinced that neither death nor life, neither angels nor demons, neither the present nor the future, nor any powers, neither height nor depth, nor anything else in all creation, will be able to separate us from the love of God that is in Christ Jesus our Lord. (Romans 8:35-39)

THE TRUTH ABOUT WORTHLESSNESS
"The Father approves of me"

1. I am handmade.

I praise you because I am fearfully and wonderfully made; your works are wonderful, I know that full well. (Psalm 139:14)

2. I am important and valuable.

I no longer call you servants, because a servant does not know his master's business. Instead, I have called you friends, for everything that I learned from my Father I have made known to you. You did not choose me, but I chose you and appointed you to go and bear fruit—fruit that will last. Then the Father will give you whatever you ask in my name. (John 15:15, 16)

In a desert land he found him, in a barren and howling waste. He shielded him and cared for him; he guarded him as the apple of his eye. (Deuteronomy 32:10)

For we are God's workmanship, created in Christ Jesus to do good works, which God prepared in advance for us to do. (Ephesians 2:10)

3. I am precious and honored in the eyes of my Father.

Since you are precious and honored in my sight, and because I love you... (Isaiah 43:4)

...for I am honored in the eyes of the LORD and my God has been my strength. (Isaiah 49:5b)

4. My life has a purpose.

And he has committed to us the message of reconciliation. We are therefore Christ's ambassadors... (2 Corinthians 5:19b-20a)

5. I am a unique creation of the Father. In all the world, there's no one else like me.

Your hands made me and formed me; give me understanding to learn your commands. (Psalm 119:73)

6. I am loved and treasured by the Creator of the universe.

The LORD appeared to us in the past, saying: "I have loved you with an everlasting love; I have drawn you with loving-kindness." (Jeremiah 31:3)

7. The Father loves me completely, thoroughly, and perfectly. There's nothing I can do to add or detract from that love.

"Though the mountains be shaken and the hills be removed, yet my unfailing love for you will not be shaken nor my covenant of peace be removed," says the LORD, who has compassion on you. (Isaiah 54:10)

...who has saved us and called us to a holy life—not because of anything we have done but because of his own purpose and grace. This grace was given us in Christ Jesus before the beginning of time, but it has now been revealed through the appearing of our Savior, Christ Jesus, who has destroyed death and has brought life and immortality to light through the gospel. (2 Timothy 1:9-10)

How great is the love the Father has lavished on us, that we should be called children of God! And that is what we are! (1 John 3:1a)

8. The Father celebrates my life! He delights in me. The Father celebrates my life! He delights in me.

The LORD your God is with you, he is mighty to save. He will take great delight in you, he will quiet you with his love, he will rejoice over you with singing. (Zephaniah 3:17)

... as a bridegroom rejoices over his bride, so will your God rejoice over you. (Isaiah 62:5b)

He brought me out into a spacious place; he rescued me because he delighted in me. (Psalm 18:19)

9. My Father loves me just as much as He loves His son, Jesus.

May they be brought to complete unity to let the world know that you sent me and have loved them even as you have loved me. (John 17:23b)

10.   I have the Father's "stamp of approval".

Do not work for food that spoils, but for food that endures to eternal life, which the Son of Man will give you. On him God the Father has placed his seal of approval. (John 6:27)

THE TRUTH ABOUT DEFILEMENT
"The Father has washed, cleaned and restored me"

1. My Father desires to restore me.

For the LORD will restore the splendor of Jacob like the splendor of Israel, even though devastators have devastated them and destroyed their vine branches. (Nahum 2:2, New American Standard Bible)

I will lead the blind by ways they have not known, along unfamiliar paths I will guide them; I will turn the darkness into light before them and make the rough places smooth. These are the things I will do; I will not forsake them. (Isaiah 42:16)

And the God of all grace, who called you to his eternal glory in Christ, after you have suffered a little while, will himself restore you and make you strong, firm and steadfast. (1 Peter 5:10-11)

2. Nothing that has happened is beyond my Father's ability to restore.

In all their distress he too was distressed, and the angel of his presence saved them. In his love and mercy he redeemed them; he lifted them up and carried them all the days of old. (Isaiah 63:9)

The LORD is my shepherd, I shall not be in want. He makes me lie down in green pastures, he leads me beside quiet waters, he restores my soul. (Psalm 23:1-3)

3. My Father can repair the damage that has been done.

I will be like the dew to Israel ; he will blossom like a lily. Like a cedar of Lebanon he will send down his roots; his young shoots will grow. His splendor will be like an olive tree, his fragrance like a cedar of Lebanon. Men will dwell again in his shade. He will flourish like the grain. He will blossom like a vine, and his fame will be like the wine from Lebanon. (Hosea 14:5-7)

'For I will restore you to health and I will heal you of your wounds,' declares the LORD , 'Because they have called you an outcast, saying: "It is Zion ; no one cares for her." (Jeremiah 30:17, New American Standard Bible)

4. My Father is the God of fresh starts and renewal.

Because of the LORD's great love we are not consumed, for his compassions never fail. They are new every morning; great is your faithfulness. (Lamentations 3:22,23)

He saved us, not because of righteous things we had done, but because of his mercy. (Titus 3:5a)

5. I have been made totally clean.

Cleanse me with hyssop, and I will be clean; wash me, and I will be whiter than snow. (Psalm 51:7)

Rejoice with Jerusalem and be glad for her, all you who love her; rejoice greatly with her. (Isaiah 66:10)

I will sprinkle clean water on you, and you will be clean; I will cleanse you from all your impurities and from all your idols. (Ezekiel 36:25)

You are already clean because of the word I have spoken to you. (John 15:3)

6. My Father has forgiven me and forgotten my sin.

For I will forgive their wickedness and will remember their sins no more. (Jeremiah 31:34b)

"Come now, let us reason together," says the LORD. "Though your sins are like scarlet, they shall be as white as snow; though they are red as crimson, they shall be like wool." (Isaiah 1:18)

7. I am chosen, treasured and loved.

Therefore, as God's chosen people, holy and dearly loved… (Colossians 3:12a)

For you are a people holy to the LORD your God. The LORD your God has chosen you out of all the peoples on the face of the earth to be his people, his treasured possession. (Deuteronomy 7:6)

The LORD appeared to us in the past, saying: "I have loved you with an everlasting love; I have drawn you with unfailing kindness." (Jeremiah 31:3)

As the Father has loved me, so have I loved you. Now remain in my love. (John 15:9)

THE TRUTH ABOUT HOPELESSNESS

"The Father has given me a living hope through Jesus"

1. The Father is trustworthy in times of difficulty.

Let us hold unswervingly to the hope we profess, for he who promised is faithful. (Hebrews 10:23)

Let the one who walks in the dark, who has no light, trust in the name of the LORD and rely on his God. (Isaiah 50:10b)

Why are you downcast, O my soul? Why so disturbed within me? Put your hope in God, for I will yet praise him, my Savior and my God. (Psalm 42:11)

2. God is always faithful, even when I'm not.

If we are faithless, he will remain faithful, for he cannot disown himself. (2 Timothy 2:13)

God is faithful, who has called you into fellowship with his Son, Jesus Christ our Lord. (1 Corinthians 1:9)

Your love, LORD, reaches to the heavens, your faithfulness to the skies. (Psalm 36:5)

3. My Father is greater than my troubles.

I have told you these things, so that in me you may have peace. In this world you will have trouble. But take heart! I have overcome the world. (John 16:33)

4. My Father's loving heart has planned help for me.

The LORD will guide you always; he will satisfy your needs in a sun-scorched land and will strengthen your frame. You will be like a well-watered garden, like a spring whose waters never fail. (Isaiah 58:11)

For I am the LORD, your God, who takes hold of your right hand and says to you, do not fear; I will help you. (Isaiah 41:13)

5. The Father makes a way for me through depression.

You, O LORD, keep my lamp burning; my God turns my darkness into light. (Psalm 18:28)

But God, who comforts the depressed, comforted us. (2 Corinthians 7:6)

6. The Father is pouring out fresh mercy for me today.

This I recall to my mind, therefore I have hope. The LORD'S loving-kindnesses indeed never cease, for His compassions never fail. They are new every morning; great is Your faithfulness. "The LORD is my portion," says my soul, "Therefore I have hope in Him." (Lamentations 3:21-24, New American Standard Bible)

Let us then approach the throne of grace with confidence, so that we may receive mercy and find grace to help us in our time of need. (Hebrews 4:16)

7. My Father's thoughts toward me are always good and filled with hope for me.

"For I know the plans I have for you," declares the LORD, "plans to prosper you and not to harm you, plans to give you hope and a future." (Jeremiah 29:11)

8. I can do all things in Christ.

I can do everything through him who gives me strength. (Philippians 4:13)

9. My Father is walking before me, preparing my way.

Forget the former things; do not dwell on the past. See, I am doing a new thing! Now it springs up; do you not perceive it? I am making a way in the desert and streams in the wasteland. (Isaiah 43:18,19)

10. The Father gives me His comfort and encouragement.

... to comfort all who mourn, and provide for those who grieve in Zion-to bestow on them a crown of beauty instead of ashes, the oil of gladness instead of mourning, and a garment of praise instead of a spirit of despair. They will be called oaks of righteousness, a planting of the LORD for the display of his splendor. (Isaiah 61:2b,3)

May our Lord Jesus Christ himself and God our Father, who loved us and by his grace gave us eternal encouragement and good hope, encourage your hearts and strengthen you in every good deed and word. (2 Thessalonians 2:16,17)

Praise be to the God and Father of our Lord Jesus Christ, the Father of compassion and the God of all comfort. (2 Corinthians 1:3)

THE TRUTH ABOUT SHAME
"I am covered with Christ"

1. My father has forgiven me and has forgotten my sin.

   If we confess our sins, he is faithful and just and will forgive us our sins and purify us from all unrighteousness. (1 John 1:9)

   I, even I, am he who blots out your transgression, for my own sake, and remembers your sins no more. (Isaiah 43:25)

2. I am totally covered.

   For all of you who were baptized into Christ have clothed yourselves with Christ. (Galatians 3:27)

   You forgave the iniquity of your people and covered all their sins. (Psalm 85:2)

   I will rejoice greatly in the Lord, my soul will exult in my God; for He has clothed me with garments of salvation, He has wrapped me with a robe of righteousness. (Isaiah 61:10, New American Standard Bible)

3. I am free from condemnation.

Therefore, there is now no condemnation for those who are in Christ Jesus, because through Christ Jesus the law of the Spirit of life set me free from the law of sin and death. (Romans 8:1,2)

4. I am enough. I am absolutely complete in Christ.

For in Christ all the fullness of the Deity lives in bodily form, and you have been given fullness in Christ, who is the head over every power and authority. (Colossians 2:9,10)

5. Jesus is not ashamed of me.

Both the one who makes men holy and those who are made holy are of the same family. So Jesus is not ashamed to call them brothers. (Hebrews 2:11)

6. The Father's thoughts towards me are always good and filled with hope for me.

"For I know the plans I have for you," declares the LORD, "plans to prosper you and not to harm you, plans to give you hope and a future." (Jeremiah 29:11)

He saved us and called us to a holy life-not because of anything we have done but because of his own purpose and grace. This grace was given us in Christ Jesus before the beginning of time. (2 Timothy 1:9)

How great is the love the Father has lavished on us, that we should be called children of God! And that is what we are! (1 John 3:1)

7. I have been made holy though Christ.

But now he has reconciled you by Christ's physical body through death to present you holy in his sight, without blemish and free from accusation. (Colossians 1:22)

God made him who had no sin to be made sin for us, so that in him we might become the righteousness of God. (2 Corinthians 5:21)

8. He sees me as beautiful, handsome, and pleasant in His eyes.

For you created my inmost being; you knit me together in my mother's womb. I praise you because I am fearfully and wonderfully make; your works are wonderful, I know that full well. (Psalm 139:13,14)

9. I am deeply loved by God.

But because of his great love for us, God, who is rich in mercy, made us alive with Christ even when we were dead in transgressions—it is by grace you have been saved. And God raised us up with Christ and seated us with him in the heavenly realms in Christ Jesus. (Ephesians 2:4-6)

10. Nothing can separate me from God's love.

For I am convinced that neither death nor life, neither angels nor demons, neither the present nor the future, nor any powers, neither height nor depth, nor anything else in all creation, will be able to separate us from the love of God that is in Christ Jesus our Lord. (Romans 8:38, 39)

MY NEW IDENTITY

Each chapter has concluded with opportunities for us to think about what we've read. Since we seek to end the book by reinforcing the reality of our new identity, we want to end differently.

We are beginning a new life. Let's end this chapter in a new way.

Review what God has stated in these chapters, in these stories, in

YOUR story. Receive your New Identity. Believe that these words which compare the former you (The Spirit of An Orphan) with the new you (The Spirit of Sonship) are words of truth.

We are no longer who we were!

We are never to remain only those people we think we can be!

We say NO to the lies!

We say YES to God's words of hope, of healing, of adoption, of acceptance, of forgiveness, of deliverance, of abundance, of adventure, of significance, of a future!

IMAGE OF GOD?

THE SPIRIT OF AN ORPHAN SAYS:

See God as Master

THE SPIRIT OF SONSHIP SAYS:

See God as a Loving Father

DEPENDENCY, THEOLOGY, SECURITY?

THE SPIRIT OF AN ORPHAN SAYS:

Independent / Self-reliant

Live by the Love of Law

Insecure / Lack peace

THE SPIRIT OF SONSHIP SAYS:

Interdependent / Acknowledges Need

Live by the Law of Love

Rest and Peace

NEED FOR APPROVAL?

THE SPIRIT OF AN ORPHAN SAYS:

Strive for the praise, approval, and acceptance of man

THE SPIRIT OF SONSHIP SAYS:

Totally accepted in God's love and justified by grace

MOTIVE BEHIND CHRISTIAN DISCIPLINES?

THE SPIRIT OF AN ORPHAN SAYS:

Duty and earning God's favor or no motivation at all

THE SPIRIT OF SONSHIP SAYS:

Pleasure and delight

MOTIVE FOR PURITY?

THE SPIRIT OF AN ORPHAN SAYS:

"Must" be holy to have God's favor, thus increasing a sense of shame and guilt

THE SPIRIT OF SONSHIP SAYS:

"Want" to be holy; do not want anything to hinder intimate relationship with God

SELF-IMAGE?

THE SPIRIT OF AN ORPHAN SAYS:

Self-rejection from comparing yourself to others

THE SPIRIT OF SONSHIP SAYS:

Positive and affirmed because you know you have such value to God

SOURCE OF COMFORT?

THE SPIRIT OF AN ORPHAN SAYS:

Seek comfort in counterfeit affections: addictions, compulsions, escapism, busyness, hyper-religious activity

THE SPIRIT OF SONSHIP SAYS:

Seek times of quietness and solitude to rest in the Father's presence and love

PEER RELATIONSHIPS?

THE SPIRIT OF AN ORPHAN SAYS:

Competition, rivalry, and jealousy toward others' success and position

THE SPIRIT OF SONSHIP SAYS:

Humility and unity as you value others and are able to rejoice in their blessings and success

HANDLING OTHERS' FAULTS?

THE SPIRIT OF AN ORPHAN SAYS:

Accusation and exposure in order to make yourself look good by making others look bad

THE SPIRIT OF SONSHIP SAYS:

Love covers as you seek to restore others in a spirit of love and gentleness

VIEW OF AUTHORITY?

THE SPIRIT OF AN ORPHAN SAYS:

See authority as a source of pain; distrustful toward them and lack a heart attitude of submission

THE SPIRIT OF SONSHIP SAYS:

Respectful, honoring; you see them as ministers of God for good in your life

VIEW OF ADMONITION?

THE SPIRIT OF AN ORPHAN SAYS:

Difficulty receiving admonition; you must be right so you easily get your feelings hurt and close your spirit to discipline

THE SPIRIT OF SONSHIP SAYS:

See the receiving of admonition as a blessing and need in your life so that your faults and weaknesses are exposed and put to death

EXPRESSION OF LOVE?

THE SPIRIT OF AN ORPHAN SAYS:

Guarded and conditional; based upon others' performance as you seek to get your own needs met

THE SPIRIT OF SONSHIP SAYS:

Open, patient, and affectionate as you lay your life and agendas down in order to meet the needs of others

SENSE OF GOD'S PRESENCE?

THE SPIRIT OF AN ORPHAN SAYS:

Conditional & Distant

THE SPIRIT OF SONSHIP SAYS:

Close & Intimate

CONDITION?

THE SPIRIT OF AN ORPHAN SAYS:

Bondage

THE SPIRIT OF SONSHIP SAYS:

Liberty

POSITION?

THE SPIRIT OF AN ORPHAN SAYS:

Feel like a Servant/Slave

THE SPIRIT OF SONSHIP SAYS:

Feel like a Son/Daughter

THE SPIRIT OF AN ORPHAN SAYS:

Spiritual ambition; the earnest desire for some spiritual achievement and distinction and the willingness to strive for it; a desire to be seen and counted among the mature

THE SPIRIT OF SONSHIP SAYS:

To daily experience the Father's unconditional love and acceptance and then be sent as a representative of His love to family and others

FUTURE?

THE SPIRIT OF AN ORPHAN SAYS:

Fight for what you can get!

THE SPIRIT OF SONSHIP SAYS:

Sonship releases your inheritance!

CONCLUSION:

A NEW IDENTITY

THROUGHOUT MY TRAVELS, I run across many people who do not know who they are. They don't know why they were created. They have heard about the life and death of Jesus, but they don't know HOW or WHY it's important to embrace Jesus as *their* Savior.

Many people are not aware that they can pray and invite God's love into their hearts. They think that because they believe in God, or they believe in any god, or they had a family member believing in God, or they attend a church, that they are going to Heaven. I explain to them that even Satan believes in God – but he isn't going to Heaven.

Whether I am ministering in the streets or in churches, people might mention a denomination, a religious background or the terminology of a church, but they know little about having a relationship with Christ. When asked about salvation and their relationship with Christ, they often have no idea of repentance, of confessing Christ aloud, of seeking forgiveness of sins, of being filled with God's Spirit. But they see there is something different about me. As they seek truth, they ask me how to become a Christian and get this new Identity.

What about you, my friend?

Where are you in your spiritual journey?

Do you know Christ personally?

Will you accept Him into your life, to rescue you from your sins and to give you a new Identity?

Or, did you have a onetime experience without an ongoing relationship with God your Father?

The truths of these pages come alive when Christ brings a new life in you – a new Identity. Please do not seek to apply these biblical principles while missing the main point: Your new Identity becomes a reality with Christ living in you.

Welcome Him. He is waiting.

To accept Christ as your Savior, ask Jesus to be the Lord of your life by praying a prayer like this: *"Jesus, I believe You died for my sins. Forgive me. Make me a new creation. Come into my heart and fill me with Your Holy Spirit."*

When you sincerely pray that prayer, remember this: It is not the end! It is the beginning of a new life. This journey of developing a new Identity is letting God lead you in the paths of righteousness. The Christ-life becomes your life. You confess Him before others. You seek to do His will.

Is it possible to live that life and do His will? Yes, but only as God's Spirit gives us the strength to live this new, amazing, healing life.

And please do not travel this journey alone. Find friends – true friends who love, accept, and forgive you as your Heavenly Father has – to walk with you.

The Identity Crisis ends. The journey with your new Identity begins. It is a journey that never ends. Enter. And enjoy.

J. Alan Hoke

> [14] *...to keep this command without spot or blame until the appearing of our Lord Jesus Christ,* [15] *which God will bring about in his own time—God, the blessed and only Ruler, the King of kings and Lord of lords,* [16] *who alone is immortal and who lives in unapproachable light, whom no one has seen or can see. To him be honor and might forever. Amen (1 Timothy 6:14-16).*

IF YOU'RE A FAN OF THIS BOOK, PLEASE TELL OTHERS...

- Write about *Identity Crisis* on your blog, Twitter, MySpace, or Facebook page

- Suggest *Identity Crisis* to friends

- When you're in a bookstore, ask them if they carry the book and if not, suggest that they order it

- Write a review of *Identity Crisis* on www.amazon.com

- Send my publisher, Higher-Life Development Services, suggestions on websites, conferences, and events you know of where this book could be offered

- Purchase additional copies to give away as gifts

CONNECT WITH ME...

To learn more about *Identity Crisis,* please contact my publisher directly:

HigherLife Development Services
2342 Westminster Terrace
Oviedo, Florida 32765
Phone: (407) 563-4806
Email: info@ahigherlife.com